A Companion to the New Testament

A Companion to the New Testament

Edited by

Michelle Fletcher and James Crossley

scm press

Published in 2024 by SCM Press
Editorial office
3rd Floor, Invicta House,
110 Golden Lane,
London EC1Y 0TG, UK
www.scmpress.co.uk

SCM Press is an imprint of Hymns Ancient & Modern Ltd
(a registered charity)

Hymns Ancient & Modern® is a registered trademark of
Hymns Ancient & Modern Ltd
13A Hellesdon Park Road, Norwich,
Norfolk NR6 5DR, UK

British Library Cataloguing in Publication data

A catalogue record for this book is available
from the British Library

978-0-334-05630-0

Typeset by Regent Typesetting

Contents

List of Contributors

James Crossley is Research Professor in Bible, Society and Politics at MF Norwegian School of Theology, Religion and Society, Oslo, Norway

Rodolfo Galvan Estrada III is the Assistant Professor of the New Testament at Vanguard University, California, USA

Michelle Fletcher is Deputy Director of the Visual Commentary on Scripture project at King's College London, UK

Michael Scott Robertson is Junior Fellow with the Beyond Canon Collaborative Research Group, Universität Regensburg, Germany

Kelsie Rodenbiker is a Research Associate at the University of Glasgow, UK and a co-investigator on the *Paratexts Seeking Understanding* project, funded by the Templeton Religion Trust

Sarah E. Rollens is an Associate Professor of Religious Studies at Rhodes College, Tennessee, USA

Isaac T. Soon is Assistant Professor of Early Christianity at the University of British Columbia, Canada

Wei Hsien Wan is an independent researcher in Kuala Lumpur, Malaysia where he also teaches writing

Introduction

Every act of reading brings a fresh interpretation to the texts which make up the New Testament. The chapters in this volume are designed to explore centuries of this reading process. It is a companion to the New Testament in the sense that it guides you through the way readers before you have read these documents. The New Testament offers a rich variety of literature, and these have been subject to an equally variegated range of reading approaches. The aim of this volume, therefore, is to expose you to different ways of engaging with New Testament literature, allowing you to see not only through the eyes of contemporary biblical scholars but also through the eyes of artists, politicians, Reformers, prophets, mathematicians, and many more.

The chapters are written by experts in New Testament interpretive history, offering you clear guidance through contested issues and complex exegetical wranglings. The authors ensure that you are aware of key debates within the current scholarly community, and foreground problematic reading strategies which have become enamelled on to New Testament interpretation. Each author takes a different approach to this task, tailoring their chapter to the specific interpretative issues which surround the book(s) being examined. This approach allows each chapter to showcase different points of interest and focus, ranging from who wrote the New Testament texts, through key theological debates and political machinations, to the concept of the 'New Testament' itself. It also allows interpretative voices from across two millennia of biblical interpretation to be heard. As a result, the strength of this volume is that the approaches it features are as diverse as the literature being read. We hope that such an approach will be particularly appealing to those looking for a dynamic guide for teaching introductory courses to the New Testament, where different approaches can be showcased including the history of the discipline, artistic reception, manuscript variations, narrative approaches, early church interpretation, and postcolonial readings.

Chapter format

Despite the variety of content, the chapters of this book follow the same format.

Each begins with a brief overview of the New Testament book(s) being explored to help you quickly grasp the focus of the texts. (The only exceptions are the two chapters on the Pauline Epistles, where the first provides an overview of all the letters together for ease of reference.) The authors then draw out and explain key themes which arise within the works, highlighting particularly pertinent points to watch out for in readings. The rest of the chapter then showcases the various readers and reading approaches. Here you will find the majority of the chapter's material, and it is here that we hope you will discover the wonder of the complex debates and readings which have preceded and shaped (and perhaps will shape) your own engagement with these texts. As already mentioned, each chapter takes a different approach in this section to address the interpretive history of the books being examined effectively. Some will explore the debates of modern biblical scholars, some will focus more on historical theological arguments, while others focus on visual legacies and fresh interpretative strategies. Many do all of this (and more!). Obviously, we cannot cover every issue, and selection and exclusion are inevitable, but we believe that the range of material in the volume provides a stimulating and informative way into these interpretative histories.

We have intentionally avoided the use of footnotes and endnotes to facilitate the reading experience. This also helps avoid any sense of a hierarchy of relevance in the material. However, should you want to explore topics further, plenty of scholarly works are referred to in the chapters and you will be able to find details of these in the References sections. In addition, each chapter concludes with a list a key literature selected by the authors for further reading.

The chapters

This book has been divided into eight chapters which reflect the diverse body of literature which makes up what is known as the New Testament. The New Testament books included in the chapters have been grouped according to the history of reading practice, allowing you to experience the ways past and present readers have engaged with collections of books as well as individual texts. As a result, works such as Revelation and the Gospel of John are treated individually due to their distinct history of interpretation, whereas the Synoptic Gospels, Pauline Epistles, and Catholic Epistles are considered as groups because they have a tradition as being viewed as what could be called 'a canon within a canon', as our authors will demonstrate.

Chapter 1 covers the Synoptic Gospels (Matthew, Mark, and Luke). Sarah E. Rollens focuses on key questions which have arisen since the earliest readers encountered these texts: what do they have in common, in what ways do they differ, and why? Shared themes, including the Kingdom, interest in the vulnerable, and attitudes to Jewish leaders are explored, as well as the unique interests of each Gospel. The chapter introduces theories which groups of academic readers have adopted to make sense of these shared and diverging documents, revealing the legacy these approaches have left for readers today. These include essential concepts such as the Synoptic Problem, the historical Jesus, and ideas about the communities who first received the documents. The chapter shows how theories have grown and fallen out of fashion and the assumptions that readers have made as they have formulated these theories. Using the historical Jesus as an example, the chapter shows how different readers see different Jesuses within these Gospels, and that different people can see opposite or even contradictory portraits. This brings to the fore the fact that every reader (ourselves included) brings their own situations and contexts to their interpretation, and that this even influences the person of Jesus 'found' within Matthew, Mark, and Luke.

In Chapter 2, Rodolfo Galvan Estrada III examines the rich and often troubling reception of the Gospel of John. He demonstrates the history of John's unique perspective by focusing on four different groups of readers: early readers, artistic receptions, modern readers, and new currents of reading. Engaging with these varying approaches to John reveals how it has made a profound impact upon the history of the Church, including the formation of its creeds, its role in shaping a negative stereotype of Jews, as well as how it has been received and interpreted by feminist, Jewish and postcolonial scholars. These readings demonstrate the importance of the connection to John the Apostle and the wide-ranging tradition of commentary writing, from the gnostic Heracleon to contemporary anti-empire readings. In doing so, the reader will be introduced to interpreters as diverse as Eusebius, Adele Reinhartz, Martin Luther, Leonardo da Vinci, Rudolf Bultmann, Clement of Alexandria, R. S. Sugirtharajah, Adolf von Harnack, and Roman catacomb painters.

The Acts of the Apostles is covered in Chapter 3 by James Crossley. This chapter demonstrates the impact that a close narrative reading of the text can have upon readerly understanding. The chapter begins by foregrounding Acts' close affinity with the Gospel of Luke, showing how key themes such as the Christian movement's connection to Judaism, the community's approach to goods, and the role of the Holy Spirit grow out of Gospel concerns. The original community that Acts addresses is then turned to, and potential clues within the text discussed. The chapter then delves deep into one of the central issues of modern Acts scholarship in a post-Holocaust world trying to come to terms with the historic legacies of anti-Judaism and antisemitism: understanding the earliest Christian movement in relation to Jews and Judaism. A close narrative reading draws out a wide range of differing interpretations, from the early church to the Venerable Bede to twenty-first-century scholarship. In doing so, it showcases both the importance of grounding readings within the narrative trajectory of Acts itself and the benefits of allowing ourselves to enter into first-century theological and social contexts. The final part of the chapter looks at the real-world ramifications of readings of Acts, including anti-Jewish interpretations, but also how the text both bolsters and challenges received power structures though the examples of imagining new social orders in England in the 1300s, Shakespearean post-Reformation reservations, and late twentieth-century Socialism.

The next two chapters are dedicated to the writings often called the 'Pauline Epistles'.

In Chapter 4, Isaac Soon introduces the reader to the person of Paul (or perhaps more accurately the many different Pauls of the New Testament), and the literature which has come to be associated with him. The chapter demonstrates how understandings of the letters and historical person of Paul have impacted textual interpretation. It traces the transmission of Pauline literature, from earliest groupings and the development of extra canonical literature to the emergence of pictorial presentations of the apostle. It then turns to focus on cutting-edge scholarship which is reassessing the reception of Paul and his letters from communities and perspectives often ignored or underexplored in Pauline reading strategies. This includes introducing readers who are using lenses such as disability, queer and gender studies, and who are recovering African-American interpretations. Thus, the legacy of reading Paul's letters is questioned and the impact these writings have on lived experience is reviewed.

In Chapter 5, Michael Scott Robertson tackles the two groups of letters which are often classed as Deutero-Pauline Epistles: 2 Thessalonians, Colossians, Ephesians, and the Pastoral Epistles (1 and 2 Timothy, and Titus). This chapter charts the history of an idea: the idea that these six letters were perhaps not written by Paul, tracing the impact this has had on current scholarly reading methods. It introduces figures instrumental to these debates, demonstrating how late eighteenth- and early nineteenth-century readers' examinations of style, language, themes and eschatology led to shifts in understanding, as well as a confidence to assert what they believed to be 'unpauline'. The chapter showcases the impact these arguments have had on readers today and asks, if not written by Paul, how could these writings claim to be by Paul and include such intimate details about him? And how do scholars posit by whom, when and where these letters were written? Key to this is the concept of pseud-epigraphy, which is lucidly summarized, before using the Pastoral Epistles to demonstrate current scholarly reading strategies and theories.

Two chapters are then dedicated to the Non-Pauline Epistles.

Chapter 6 focuses on Hebrews, with Michelle Fletcher and Wei Hsien Wan guiding readers through its impact on Christian thought and practice. Authorship of Hebrews has always been contested and so manuscripts from the fourth to the twelfth century are used to uncover its complicated relationship with the person of Paul. The chapter also shows how Hebrews has had a central role in key theological battles throughout church history, unpacking complex interpretive debates and heated disputes. It showcases the role of Hebrews 1 in the Arian controversy, the place of Hebrews 6 in the Nestorian apostasy schism, the import of Hebrews 7 for Reformers' understandings of the priesthood, and the problematic use of Hebrews 8—12's language of 'shadow' and 'better' in the complicated history of Jewish–Christian relations. Finally, the chapter demonstrates how Hebrews is very much alive in the lived experience of the church and that, despite its non-narrative nature, it has generated fascinating artistic responses, including Russian icons, Dutch engravings, and a series of paintings by New Zealand artist Colin McCahon.

The Catholic Epistles are the focus of Chapter 7 by Kelsie Rodenbiker. This chapter explores the process of readerly understanding which led to these seven letters becoming known as the Catholic Epistles. This involves tracing their earliest reception by church fathers and examining the material evidence that led to their eventual canonization. A particular focus for this chapter is the way that understandings in the minds of readers come about, even if this might be at odds with the evidence being presented. After all, why should we understand these seven letters as a collection if there is no clear, historical tie between their production? The chapter reveals shared themes and interests within the corpus including faithful works, stability, and concern over the last days. The concerns of modern scholarly readers are also explored, revealing the importance of connecting these documents with the apostles, and the multiple 'Peters' and 'Johns' who haunt their pages as a result. Ultimately, this chapter shows how the presence of this corpus within the New Testament troubles and exerts influence by causing readers to ask, what really is canonical?

Chapter 8 considers the book of Revelation. Michelle Fletcher brings together a host of readers to showcase the varied and rich reception history of the book from the earliest church to the present day. From North African commentaries to English mathematical calculations, from American female prophets to illuminated manuscripts, from South African anti-apartheid writings to the Geneva Bible, and from the Easter liturgy of the Coptic Church to the world's largest aluminium statue, this chapter reveals how Revelation's readers have interpreted its world-shaking narratives in their own, localized contexts. Along the way, key Revelation-related issues such as the Antichrist, the rapture, recapitulation, and the afterlife are encountered, as well as perennial interpretative questions such as: What do its claims about being a prophecy mean for the future? What do the strange host of characters contained within it symbolise? And how does it speak to the church in the here and now?

Collectively, these chapters present an exciting new companion to the writings of the Christian Testament, introducing you to readers from the first century to the twenty-first, ensuring that you are aware of key debates within historic and current scholarship, and highlighting the varied legacies generated by these texts.

Isaac T. Soon points out in his chapter that there is no substitute for a careful reading of each of these New Testament texts. This is indeed true. However, we hope that this companion to the New Testament will provide you with a wealth of different perspectives which allow you to see the texts in new ways, to find out about the experiences of readers who have encountered these works before you, and to have a fresh awareness of the debates which have enlivened New Testament reading through the centuries.

Michelle Fletcher and James Crossley

I

The Synoptic Gospels

SARAH E. ROLLENS

If asked to describe the 'core' of the New Testament, most people would probably point to the stories of Jesus' life. As many readers will know, there are four versions of the life of Jesus in the New Testament, so the notion of a 'core' to the New Testament is slightly more complex than it first appears. These narrative accounts are known as Gospels, and although there are only four Gospels in the New Testament canon – the so-called 'canonical' Gospels – there are some 30 others that existed in antiquity, termed 'non-canonical' or 'extra-canonical'. Decisions about which books should be included in the New Testament were made by church leaders (often after contentious debates) long after each of these documents was penned; therefore, if a text was not included in the New Testament, it does not mean that it was not widely read or theologically important to some early Christians.

The term 'Gospel' derives from an ancient Greek word that simply means 'good news' and, accordingly, each of these four stories outlines what it considers to be the 'good news' about the life and teachings of Jesus. Three of these Gospels are strikingly similar and are the focus of this chapter: the Gospels of Matthew, Mark, and Luke. As the canonical Gospels are anonymous, the names that we now associate with them were ascribed by later Christian thinkers. (For simplicity, this chapter still refers to each as Matthew, Mark, and Luke and uses the pronoun 'he' for their authors.) Biblical scholars deem these Gospels 'Synoptic' Gospels, which derives from the Greek word meaning 'to see together'. When compared with one another, the Synoptic Gospels contain a high degree of similarity in terms of content and writing style, which suggests that there is likely a literary relationship among them. The remaining canonical Gospel (John) is excluded from this categorization, differing in writing style and chronological sequence from the Synoptics. The Gospel of John, therefore, is discussed in Chapter 2.

This chapter showcases key scholarly theories about the Synoptic Gospels. The literary relationship between the three Gospels is known as the Synoptic Problem, and we shall see that it takes careful study to 'solve', that is, to *explain* the literary relationship among these Gospels. Solving the Synoptic Problem is only one aspect of studying the Synoptics though; this chapter shows how we can also consider the central themes of each individual Gospel and those that they share with each other. It also demonstrates the importance of the academic reception of the Synoptic Gospels, that is, how scholars have put these texts to work to help understand earliest Christianity. Therefore, after a brief overview of the Synoptic Gospels and a discussion of their key themes (those shared by all and those unique to each), this chapter presents some of the major scholarly theories which surround the study of these Gospels. This is of particular importance because, since the three Gospels are not identical accounts, scholars can examine each to discern what information the author was interested in and what portrait of Jesus they wanted to promote. In other words, we shall see how, even if there is a singular 'core' story to the New Testament, it has developed and expanded in all manner of ways.

Overview of the Synoptic Gospels

Two of the Synoptic Gospels, Matthew and Luke, begin with the early life of Jesus, the so-called Infancy Narratives. These include the famous genealogies of Jesus, as well as the stories surrounding his birth that inform Christmas nativity scenes. But neither Matthew nor Luke is deeply interested in Jesus' youth. After introducing the few stories associated with his birth, they both jump straight to his baptism, which most scholars agree happened around the time that he was 30 years old. The Gospel of Mark, thought to be written first (more on this later), neglects *any* details of Jesus' early life and simply begins with his baptism.

In all the Synoptics, following his baptism Jesus then begins his teaching career, which takes him throughout Galilee, a Roman province in the first century AD, and the surrounding regions. Most scholars suppose that this public preaching lasted about a year. It is in this portion of the Synoptic Gospels that we find some of Jesus' most well-known teachings. All three of the Synoptics, for instance, preserve a version of the Parable of the Mustard Seed (Matt. 13.31–32; Mark 4.30–32; Luke 13.18–19). Matthew and Luke contain similar, though not identical, versions of the Sermon on the Mount (or the Plain in Luke's account), and two different versions of the Lord's Prayer (Matt. 6.9–15; Luke 11.1–4). The Synoptics all describe Jesus' unexpected transfiguration before a handful of his disciples (Mark 9.2–9; Matt. 17.1–9; Luke 9.28–36). While travelling throughout Galilee and elsewhere, Jesus demonstrates his power through various miracles (for example, Mark 4.35–41; Matt. 14.22–27; 21.18–20) and through the healing of unwell people (for example, Mark 3.1–6; Luke 5.12–14, 17–26). Both bolster his reputation among the local villagers but also lead to various conflicts with Jewish leaders, such as Pharisees, Sadducees, and scribes. Eventually, the Synoptics depict Jesus winding up his regional activity in Galilee and turning with his disciples towards Judea, with its capital Jerusalem, where he lives out his last week. The final chapters of the Synoptics depict Jesus' increasing conflict with Jerusalem authorities, his arrest in the Garden of Gethsemane, his trial before Pilate, and his public crucifixion.

The Synoptics differ on what happened after Jesus' death. In the earliest version of the Gospel of Mark, Mark 16 ended at the verse where the three women who had come to Jesus' tomb find it empty and flee from fear (Mark 16.8); Mark did not contain any description of Jesus appearing to his disciples or any sense of how the movement that Jesus began was sustained by his followers. Since this is an abrupt ending that leaves many open questions – indeed, the question of what happened to Jesus after his death is ambiguous in Mark – later scribes added verses 9–20 to append a more satisfying ending and to bring the Gospel more in line with Matthew and Luke, which contain more elaborate endings. Matthew relates that the women saw Jesus on their way to tell the other disciples about the empty tomb (Matt. 28.8–10) and that Jesus' final act after his resurrection was to commission his disciples to carry on his work (Matt. 28.16–20). Luke's ending is even more detailed. It includes two different stories in which Jesus' followers see him after his death and resurrection (Luke 24.13–32, 33–49), and it also depicts Jesus ascending to heaven in front of his disciples (Luke 24.50–51).

Themes in the Synoptic Gospels

Shared theme: Against Jewish leaders

All three Gospels are interested in pitting Jesus' authority against that of Jewish leaders. Centuries of antisemitic proponents have misinterpreted the Gospel narratives, assuming they depicted Jesus and his followers as singularly against 'the Jews', as an entire ethnic and religious group (see Chapter 2). However, a closer textual analysis reveals that many Jewish people were sincerely interested in Jesus and his activity. Indeed, Jesus, all his disciples, and most of his first followers were Jewish. The Synoptics present his major conflicts with Jewish *leaders*. For instance, in Matthew 23 Jesus takes aim at the scribes and Pharisees for their supposedly flawed interpretation of the law. Likewise, Luke 14.1–6 and Mark 2.23–28 depict Jesus in conflict with the Pharisees over proper Sabbath observance. Thus, Jesus may have found himself set against certain Jewish leaders, but many of the local Jewish villagers had no problem entertaining his teachings, and were happy to be the beneficiaries of his miracle working.

However, the conflict with Jewish leaders is understandable. What Jesus is remembered as doing (that is, making judgements about aspects of Jewish law) challenged the authority of many of those leaders (see Mark 3.1–6; Luke 13.10–17). Jesus' healings of people with certain illnesses, especially those involving bodily discharge, potentially circumvented some purity practices outlined in Leviticus that some Jewish authorities emphasized for proper healing (see Luke 8.43–48). The conflict that Jesus has with *specific* Jewish figures in these narratives crops up in *specific* locations and over *specific* issues. It was never intended to portray Jesus as set in opposition to the entire religion of Judaism, as the interpretations and practices he recommends are entirely expected within the diverse expressions of Judaism we know existed in his time (see Sanders 1977 and 1985).

Shared theme: John the Baptist

All three Gospels are keen to relate the movement surrounding Jesus to that begun by John the Baptist. Before Jesus starts his public teaching, he goes to the Jordan River to be baptized. Mark says explicitly that John the Baptist carried out his baptism (Mark 1.9). However, this incident may have raised some questions for later readers: Why does Jesus need to be baptized by John? Does this imply that he has sins that need to be cleansed? Does this mean that Jesus is inferior to John? By the time Matthew composed his version, he inserted a brief dialogue into Mark's baptism narrative, allowing Jesus the opportunity to explain that his baptism by John must be done 'to fulfil all righteousness' (Matt. 3.13–15). Luke uses a different tactic to deal with this problem. In the passage before Jesus' baptism, he states that John was put in prison by Herod Antipas and in the narration of the baptism uses the passive voice (Jesus 'was baptized', Luke 3.21) to disguise the agent. Despite this, Luke is still keen to affiliate Jesus and John. Unlike the other Synoptics, Luke includes stories that suggest that Jesus and John are biologically related and that their mothers' pregnancies overlapped (Luke 1).

At the very least, we may surmise that the association between Jesus and John was important enough for the Synoptic authors to address it explicitly within their stories.

Shared theme: The kingdom

Perhaps the most central motif in Jesus' preaching across the Synoptics is the concept of the kingdom (or reign) of God. (John rarely uses this terminology, which further supports the categorization of the Synoptics as apart from John.) The kingdom of God resists a simplistic definition. Rather, it is described in numerous ways across the Synoptics, and many passages can be interpreted in different ways simultaneously. Indeed, I have argued that the multiple meanings of the term might be one of the attractions to using it (Rollens, 2014, pp. 178–85; see also Vaage, 1995, p. 220).

In some passages, the kingdom of God seems to refer to an *eschatological destination* and a physical space that one can enter. An example of this can be found in the Parable of the Great Banquet (Luke 14.15–24). Since the kingdom of God is depicted as a banquet that people can attend, we can surmise that many ancient people believed that the kingdom occupied a physical space and that it was a place that one could hope to go in the future if deemed worthy (as in Matt. 19.23–26).

Elsewhere, the kingdom of God appears to be more of a *present reality*, something akin to realizing God's reign on earth. Indeed, many ancient Jews expected the kingdom of God to appear at any moment (Luke 19.11). For instance, in Luke's Gospel Jesus tells his disciples to inform the recipients of the healing that 'the kingdom of God has come near to you' (Luke 10.9). This suggests that through the disciples' actions, they are able to bring the kingdom to life, so to speak, on earth.

Some argue that the kingdom should be understood as the communal expression of the providence of God and the ethical behaviour that Jesus taught; a kind of social programme embodied within the followers of Jesus, as found in Matthew 6.25–34 and Luke 12.22–32. Here, the kingdom stands for a way of life in which one's basic needs are all miraculously met by God. It is almost akin to living according to nature. Such an interpretation might make sense of the rather enigmatic statement in Luke 17.21: 'behold, the kingdom of God is among you.' The kingdom here could be a social reality expressed through the community of Jesus' followers.

In other cases, the kingdom of God/heaven resists clear articulation. Consider Luke 13.21, where Jesus likens the kingdom to 'yeast that a woman took and mixed in with three measures of flour until all of it was leavened.' The kingdom evidently spreads and infects that with which it comes into contact, but its nature is unclear. One cannot even tell if it is a good thing or a bad thing from such a concise parable.

The Synoptics share an interest in the kingdom of God as a central theme of Jesus' teaching. Although it might be challenging to decode what it refers to in every instance, at the very least it is clear that the authors agreed that the kingdom of God featured significantly in his discourse.

Unique themes: Mark

Mark is infamous for promoting the theme of Jesus' consistently misunderstood identity. Biblical scholars have long noticed that Jesus in Mark refuses to explain his identity to those he encounters until the very end of his life (14.61–62). Until that moment, if any character would guess that Jesus was the 'Son of God' or the 'Messiah', he would demand that they not tell anyone (1.25, 34, 44; 3.12). Mark does not confirm Jesus' divine identity for the reader until the centurion's climactic statement: 'Truly this was man was God's Son!' (15.39). In short, Mark is clear that from the beginning of his teaching activities, Jesus' identity befuddled those he came in contact with – and for good reason, too: Jesus himself intended his identity to be kept a secret. By the time Matthew and Luke adapted Mark's narrative, they both emphasized that Jesus' remarkable, messianic identity was evident to others, even when he was a child.

Unique themes: Matthew

Matthew is keen to represent Jesus as an authoritative interpreter of Mosaic law. For instance, Matthew's Jesus makes the famous pronouncement that he 'has not come to abolish the law and the prophets ... but to fulfil them' (5.17). Later, Matthew juxtaposes Jesus' authority to teach with that of traditional Jewish authorities: Jesus spoke as 'one having authority, and not as their scribes' (7.29). These statements are not found in the other Synoptic Gospels. The Gospel of Matthew is also unique in including the so-called antitheses in Matthew 5.21–44, which present Jesus as giving new interpretations of teachings found in Mosaic law. This means that Matthew understood the law to be central to his understanding of Jesus' movement. Importantly, Matthew's antitheses (and other passages such as 23.1–26) still recommend adhering to Mosaic law even though the traditional interpreters of it are rendered problematic.

Finally, many scholars think that Matthew deliberately modelled Jesus on Moses by having him give his major teaching speech on a mountain: Exodus says Moses received the major teachings of the law on a mountain.

In all these ways, Matthew consistently portrays Jesus as a figure who has something important to say about Jewish law.

Unique themes: Luke

One of the more intriguing emphases found in Luke is the interest in what we might today call 'social justice'. The Roman Empire was built on innate social inequality and, accordingly, 'social justice' was not a concept that ancient people would have been familiar with. Even though social justice is thus anachronistic in this context, we can still observe how Luke seems more interested than the other Synoptic authors in portraying Jesus as helping the most defenceless people in society. For instance, Jesus heals a woman who had been 'bent over' (13.11) for 18 years. Such a person was doubly vulnerable in the Roman world: a woman in a patriarchal system, and a disabled person in a society that valued physical ability and strength, while suspecting that infirmities resulted from character flaws or spirit possession. The portrayal of Jesus healing and placing his hands upon such a woman (13.13) indicates that Luke was sensitive to the plight of such people and interested in depicting them as accepted by the Jesus movement. The Parable of the Good Samaritan (10.29–37) is similar, as elevating a Samaritan to one who should be emulated suggests that conventional social valuation was being questioned. A final example is the Parable of the Rich Man and Lazarus (16.19–31). The fact that the fate of each is explored in the afterlife suggests that Luke was interested in calling some conventional attitudes into question. (For example, that God regards wealthy people as inherently better or more valuable than others.)

In some sense, Luke's interest in such figures is curious, given his sophisticated writing style suggests that he was likely not one of the vulnerable in society (Luke 1.1). Nevertheless, those vulnerable people came to his attention far more frequently than they did for the other Synoptic authors.

This discussion of themes illustrates how the Synoptics share a basic core story, but nevertheless distinguish themselves with distinct emphases. This is precisely what we would expect when we acknowledge that they were written at different times and places by authors who had different intellectual projects for different audiences.

Reception: Modern biblical scholarship and memories of the historical Jesus

The Synoptic Problem

Many readers do not realize the extent of the Synoptic similarities because they read the Gospels one at a time. However, biblical scholars use a special research tool known as a *synopsis* that aligns the Gospels side by side to make comparison easier. Through this comparison, anyone reading these three Gospels would be struck by their close similarity, and occasionally verbatim agreement in certain passages.

The earliest readers noted similarities, and debates have arisen regarding which Gospel came first. The relationship between the Synoptics was one of the most prominent discussions in the emergence of modern biblical scholarship in the late eighteenth and nineteenth centuries. Following the lead of Johann Jakob Griesbach (1745–1812) an early solution to the problem was the claim that Matthew was written first, Luke then used Matthew, and Mark in turn used both. This is known as the Two-Gospel Hypothesis and has since fallen out of fashion. (For more, see Dungan, 2007).

Solving the Synoptic Problem involves exceptionally detailed, textually based arguments, and it is not possible to engage in such analysis here. (For those curious, the required reading on the topic is John S. Kloppenborg's *Excavating Q* (2000).)

Briefly, however, in the Synoptic 'solution' that most modern scholars believe explains the Gospels' similarities, it is commonly held that Mark, the shortest Gospel with the least sophisticated writing style, was the earliest Gospel written. Since Mark was lacking in both style and content, most New Testament scholars believe that Matthew and Luke used Mark as an outline for their Gospels. They followed his basic story, improving his writing style along the way, and supplemented it with some other material that they knew, such as the Lord's Prayer and some new parables. Where did they get their extra material? Synoptic comparison reveals that this material often agrees very closely in Matthew and Luke, even though it appears at different points in their stories. It almost seems as if they were consulting *another* source in addition to Mark. Indeed, many Synoptic scholars maintain that Matthew and Luke each worked independently and used Mark, along with another written source, to compose their Gospels. This 'solution' to the Synoptic Problem is known as the Two-Source Hypothesis.

The second source is only hypothetical, that is, it can be inferred based on strong verbal similarities between Matthew and Luke. Scholars refer to this second source as 'Q' which is an abbreviation of the German term *Quelle* ('source'). Q was likely a collection of Jesus' sayings (about 235 verses) that circulated independently of any narrative of Jesus' life. It has been reconstructed based on the shared wording in Matthew and Luke, and the result is James Robinson, Paul Hoffmann and John Kloppenborg's *The Critical Edition of Q* (2000). The hypothetical Q would represent one of the earliest texts produced by the followers of Jesus and, intriguingly, embodies an expression of the Jesus movement that, though familiar with his death, did not privilege it for its theology or require a narrative representation of it. And though it is only 'hypothetical', it is a *strong* hypothesis, based as it is on similar passages that are found in Matthew and Luke but not in Mark.

There are also other possible ways to conceptualize this literary relationship, although they are not as common as the Two-Source Hypothesis. One popular explanation holds that Mark was the first Gospel to be written, Matthew used Mark to compose his Gospel, and Luke used both Matthew and Mark.

Communities

On their own, the Synoptic Gospels give us the stories of Jesus that three different authors wanted to promote. Older New Testament scholarship (pre-2010) was often fixated on situating each the Gospels within a distinct 'community', imagining it written for a community of people and responding to its concerns. It was (and for many, still is) considered accurate to speak of 'Matthew's community' or 'Mark's community'. The assumption was that an author was embedded in a distinct Christian group and that they penned a text which reflected the unique concerns of his group. Thus, many argued that Mark's community was wrestling with community identity and other related issues in the Jesus movement during or after the Jewish war with Rome, and that Mark's theme of consistent misunderstanding of Jesus' identity, even among his own disciples, was seen to justify why the movement did not flourish as quickly as their community had hoped. (For examples of this argument, see Mack, 1988; Arnal, 2008; Wright, 2023; Parrish, 2023).

However, the method of using a text as a window into a community is now widely held to be a relatively unsophisticated form of analysis (see, for example, Stowers, 2011). The assumption that the ideas in a text reflect a coherent community of believers has roots in both German Romanticism and the Protestant Reformation, both of which assumed that a social group could be known by the set of beliefs that it expressed (see Rollens, 2019). In fact, as Robyn Faith Walsh (2021) has argued, given what is known about ancient writing practices, it seems more likely that the authors were literate figures who were participating in a network of other intellectuals and cultural producers. It is unwise to try to extrapolate from the rhetorical level any robust theories about a community that may or may not have engaged with the text. In addition, the notion that authors are mere spokespeople for groups in which they are embedded is too simplistic. Intellectuals have all manner of relationships to the social group out of which they arise, and so we must consider a variety of forms of mediation between text and social constituency (Rollens, 2014, pp. 44–79).

Historical Jesus

How the Synoptic Gospels have figured in theological, social, cultural, and political projects in the centuries, even millennia that have followed, is known as reception history. Reception history charts how people have created meaning by using and reusing these texts and the ideas contained within them. In thinking about how these Gospels have been interpreted over the centuries, one fascinating site for discussion is scholarship on the historical Jesus. By briefly considering how these Gospels have functioned within efforts to reconstruct the historical person of Jesus, we can see how people have received these texts and made them work for differing cultural locations.

The Synoptic Gospels relate the story of Jesus' life and death, and they are the primary sources that scholars have for knowing anything about the historical Jesus – though admittedly scholars approach them with different levels of confidence regarding how well these texts reflect the real person of Jesus. Unfortunately for scholars, the Gospels are not disinterested, historical reports; they are theologically interested and politically motivated documents. As we have seen above, this means that even as they present an account of a person who lived in Galilee over 2,000 years ago, they also embed within that story their own theological beliefs and assumptions about how the world works.

But we must first ground this discussion in an important realization: ancient people were not interested in the historical Jesus. Such a statement is deliberately provocative, so it is necessary to unpack its meaning before turning to the modern enterprise of reconstructing the historical Jesus. By suggesting that ancient people were not interested in the historical Jesus, I am proposing that they did not look to the Gospels with our modern, analytical lenses to discern which parts really go back to Jesus and which were later 'inventions' or 'additions' by his followers. It is this which has been a preoccupation of modern readers. The stories about Jesus emerged in a cultural context full of similar stories about other gods and divine beings, and their truth or falsehood was not something that most ancient people were interested in regularly assessing. After all, most of the Roman Empire had no trouble accepting that Augustus, the first emperor, became a god upon his death. There was no compelling reason to doubt such a thing – just as there was no reason to doubt that the Jewish God could decide to have a son with a mortal, Galilean woman and that the son could grow up to become a wonder-working teacher.

After the Enlightenment, an intellectual revolution which emphasized the seemingly objective authority of science and other human-centred disciplines, modern biblical scholars developed interests in the Gospels that differed a great deal from the ancients. Nearly from its inception, modern biblical scholarship was preoccupied with *origins*, namely, explaining where various sayings and stories in the Gospels came from. Were they authentic teachings of Jesus? Were they invented by later Christians? If the latter, when and why? If the former, to what extent can we reconstruct the complete life and teachings of this historical person? For those who work on historical Jesus scholarship, the Synoptic Gospels (in particular, Mark and Q) are the best evidence that we have for this person. Rather than make an argument for a particular portrait of Jesus, the final section of this chapter will illustrate *how* the Synoptic Gospels have been used differently to support rather different notions of who Jesus was. At the very least, this should cause us to pause and ask how it can be that such a limited range of texts can yield such a diversity of views.

Several portraits of Jesus have been based all or in large measure on the Q source alone, on the assumption that it is the earliest, and thus the most accurate, representation of Jesus' life and teachings. The general portrait of Jesus that emerges if one treats the Q source as the best evidence for him is one that we might generally call a 'wisdom sage'. Jesus the wisdom sage is remembered primarily for his wise, ethical teachings, many of which embody countercultural perspectives. This is the reconstruction of the historical Jesus that was preferred and promoted by the Jesus Seminar, a collaborative group of scholars who worked in the 1980s and 1990s on reconstructing a definitive portrait of Jesus. Such a depiction of Jesus based on the Q source features strongly in John Dominic Crossan's *The Historical Jesus* (1991), Burton L. Mack's *The Lost Gospel* (1993), and James Robinson's *The Gospel of Jesus* (2005). The best examples of Jesus the wisdom sage's wise teachings are found in Q's Sermon, which contains classic teachings on non-judgement and non-retaliation. Many of Jesus' sayings in Q also embody a sense of reversal and the accusation that the conventional values of his ancient interlocutors are distorted or even backward altogether. Q 6.20–21, for instance, blesses those who are poor and have hunger; Jesus promises that they will inherit the kingdom of God, as opposed to the wealthy and powerful. As we have seen above, this rubs up against typical social valuation in Roman society, which assumed that wealthy people were necessarily better than others and that they deserved their wealth. Jesus also challenges social norms in Q 14.26, where he pronounces that one cannot be his disciple unless they are prepared to hate their family. This is probably an exaggerated statement that acknowledges the social conflicts that might come to a person for their involvement in the Jesus movement. Interestingly, many scholars have observed that these countercultural attitudes are quite similar to ones found among ancient Cynic philosophers (see Goulet-Cazé, 2019; Mack, 1993; Vaage, 1994).

Any reconstruction of Jesus that is based solely on Q will automatically lack something: a focus on Jesus' death. The scholarly reconstruction of Q has no passion narrative, and although the Q sayings are aware of Jesus' death, it does not feature heavily in the text. The result is that the historical Jesus, when reconstructed from Q, is important more for his teachings than his salvific death. As one might imagine, this is difficult for many people familiar with the theological import of his death to understand. The dominant forms of Christianity have long held that Jesus' death is the single most important thing that he did. But Q (and other texts such as the Gospel of Thomas) suggests that not all ancient people focused on that. Instead they remembered him primarily as a teacher of ethics and wisdom.

The 'rival' reconstruction of the historical Jesus to that of a wisdom sage is that of an apocalyptic or messianic prophet – a portrait of Jesus that features centrally his unjust death. This reconstruction uses some sayings from Q, but it also draws extensively on evidence from the other canonical Gospels. Proponents of this reconstruction emphasize that Jesus understood himself to be on a mission from God and that his task was to warn people of God's impending destruction if they did not change their ways. Such a view of Jesus was encapsulated famously in Albert Schweitzer's *The Quest of the Historical Jesus* (1906), but it remains popular today. Bart D. Ehrman, for instance, has argued extensively for this portrait of Jesus in his *Jesus: Apocalyptic Prophet of the New Millennium* (1999). As an apocalyptic prophet, Jesus was pessimistic about the current state of the world and literally expected God to show up at any moment to set things right for his people. This stands in stark tension with the notion of Jesus as a wisdom sage. As a wisdom sage, Jesus was interested in educating people into a proper understanding of the world and in helping them intervene in society to make a more just, egalitarian and virtuous mode of existence, but as an apocalyptic prophet, Jesus saw no hope among humanity and appealed instead for divine intervention. Thus, we can clearly see that some scholarly reconstructions are fundamentally at odds with one another. Such a tension is evident in the remarks of Paula Fredriksen in her *Jesus of Nazareth, King of the Jews* (1999). According to Fredriksen:

> The Jesus encountered in the present reconstruction is a prophet who preached the coming apocalyptic Kingdom of God. His message coheres both with that of his predecessor and mentor, John the Baptizer, and with that of the movement that sprang up in his name. This Jesus thus is *not* primarily a social reformer with a revolutionary message; nor is he a religious innovator radically redefining the traditional ideas and practices of his native religion. His urgent message had not the present so much as the near future in view. (p. 266)

It is not just that Fredriksen's understanding of Jesus as an apocalyptic prophet is *different* than that of other scholars, but it is also *incompatible* with them. This debate is all the more fascinating when we keep in mind that all scholars are working with the same, rather limited, collection of ancient sources.

These two reconstructions of the historical Jesus are a mere selection of the numerous portraits of Jesus that modern scholars have constructed from the Synoptic Gospels. Scholars of early Christianity have proposed many others, including Jesus the Exorcist, Jesus the Rabbi, Jesus the Feminist, or Jesus the Revolutionary. This immediately raises the question of which one is 'right' (and also how to navigate the multiple disagreements among them). This may be an unanswerable question, especially since the criteria that scholars used to rely on to assess the historical evidence have been subject to serious critique of late (for example Le Donne and Keith, 2012).

To complicate matters further, many scholars have become increasingly sceptical of the enterprise of reconstructing the historical Jesus, for several important reasons. First, biblical scholars, following trends in the study of history more broadly, are frequently suspicious about the ability to reconstruct a single person and their personality from texts alone. Second and related, there is also an increasing awareness of theological and political aims of early Christian texts, which preclude our ability to treat them as neutral histories. As stated above, they are political and ideological projects, not unbiased records of history. Third, biblical scholars have turned to memory studies to persuasively argue that the evidence that exists in the Gospels is not mere historical data but, rather, carefully crafted individual and collective memories – memories which have been transformed to serve particular purposes within the Gospels (for example see Kirk, 2018; Keith, 2011). Whether those memories reflect actual, historical events or people is challenging.

How, then, can the Synoptics be used to help scholars understand the origins of Christianity? We have seen that they show us the *range* of diverse perspectives that followers of Jesus had regarding his identity. At the same time, they also show us how different authors used varying intellectual resources to create their literary products. To offer one example in closing: scholars have recently shown how the author of Matthew's Gospel draws on ideas from Stoicism, a Greek philosophical school of thought, to discuss topics related to morality (for more see, Stowers, 2010). In this case, we do not learn much about the historical Jesus himself, but we can come to know something of the intellectual influences that determined the form his teachings took in Matthew's Gospel.

In sum, Synoptic scholarship sees each of the three Gospels as interesting in their own right for the perspective that they offer on the life of Jesus. It may be challenging to sift through their similarities and differences to discern a historical core that accurately reflects the historical figure of Jesus, but this has not deterred countless scholars from trying. No matter how one approaches these Gospels, they offer us a window into the formative stages of Christianity and into some of the earliest attempts to write about the life of Jesus. They are thus, as part of the canon of Scripture, invaluable instances of early Christians devoting intellectual energy and skills to this emerging movement.

Recommended further reading

Goodacre, Mark, 2001, *The Synoptic Problem: A Way Through the Maze*, London: T&T Clark.

Kloppenborg, John S., 2000, *Excavating Q: The History and Setting of the Sayings Gospel*, Minneapolis, MN: Fortress Press.

Mack, Burton L., 1988, *A Myth of Innocence: Mark and Christian Origins*, Philadelphia, PA: Fortress Press.

Robinson, James M., 2005, *The Gospel of Jesus: In Search of the Original Good News*, San Francisco, CA: HarperOne.

Walsh, Robyn Faith, 2021, *The Beginnings of Gospel Literature*, Cambridge: Cambridge University Press.

References

Arnal, William E., 2008, 'The Gospel of Mark as Reflection on Exile and Identity', in Willi Braun and Russell T. McCutcheon (eds), *Introducing Religion*, London: Equinox, pp. 57–67.

Crossan, John Dominic, 1991, *The Historical Jesus: The Life of a Mediterranean Jewish Peasant*, San Francisco, CA: HarperCollins.

Dungan, David, 2007, *A History of the Synoptic Problem: The Canon, the Text, the Composition, and the Interpretation of the Gospels*, New Haven, CT: Yale University Press.

Ehrman, Bart D., 1999, *Jesus, Apocalyptic Prophet of the New Millennium*, Oxford: Oxford University Press.

Fredriksen, Paula, 1999, *Jesus of Nazareth, King of the Jews: A Jewish Life and the Emergence of Christianity*, London: Macmillan.

Goulet-Cazé, Marie-Odile, 2019, *Cynicism and Christianity in Antiquity*, Grand Rapids, MI: Eerdmans.

Keith, Chris, 2011, 'Memory and Authenticity. Jesus Tradition and What Really Happened', *Zeitschrift Für Die Neutestamentliche Wissenschaft Und Die Kunde Der Älteren Kirche*, 102 2, pp. 155–77.

Kirk, Alan, 2018, *Memory and the Jesus Tradition, Reception of Jesus in the First Three Centuries*, London: Bloomsbury T&T Clark.

Kloppenborg, John S., 2000, *Excavating Q: The History and Setting of the Sayings Gospel*, Minneapolis, MN: Fortress Press.

Le Donne, Anthony and Chris Keith (eds), 2012, *Jesus, Criteria, and the Demise of Authenticity*, London: T&T Clark.

Mack, Burton L., 1988, *A Myth of Innocence: Mark and Christian Origins*, Philadelphia, PA: Fortress Press.

———, 1993, *The Lost Gospel: The Book of Q and Christian Origins*, San Francisco, CA: HarperCollins.

Parrish, John W., 2023, '"After This, Nothing Happened": Historical Vulnerability and the End of (Cultural) Time in the Gospel of Mark', in Sarah E. Rollens and Patrick Hart (eds), *Worth More Than Many Sparrows: Essays in Honor of Willi Braun*, London: Equinox, pp. 220–37.

Robinson, James M., 2005, *The Gospel of Jesus: In Search of the Original Good News*, San Francisco, CA: HarperOne.

Robinson, James M., Paul Hoffmann and John S. Kloppenborg (eds), 2000, *The Critical Edition of Q: A Synopsis Including the Gospels of Matthew and Luke, Mark and Thomas with English with German and French Translations of Q and Thomas*, Hermeneia Supplement Series, Minneapolis, MN: Fortress Press.

Rollens, Sarah E., 2014, *Framing Social Criticism in the Jesus Movement: The Ideological Project in the Sayings Gospel Q*, Tübingen: Mohr Siebeck.

———, 2019, 'The Anachronism of "Early Christian Communities"', in Nickolas P. Roubekas (ed.), *Theorizing 'Religion' in Antiquity*, Studies in Ancient Religion and Culture, Sheffield: Equinox, pp. 307–24.

Sanders, E. P., 1977, *Paul and Palestinian Judaism: A Comparison of Patterns of Religion*, Minneapolis, MN: Fortress Press.

———, 1985, *Jesus and Judaism*, Philadelphia, PA: Fortress Press.

Schweitzer, Albert, 1906, *Von Reimarus Zu Wrede: Eine Geschichte Der Leben-Jesu-Forschung*, Tübingen: J. C. B. Mohr (Paul Siebeck).

Stowers, Stanley K., 2010, 'Jesus as Teacher and Stoic Ethics in the Gospel of Matthew', in Ismo Dundenberg, Troels Engberg-Pedersen, and Tuomas Rasimus (eds), *Stoicism in Early Christianity*, Peabody: Hendrickson.

———, 2011, 'The Concept of "Community" and the History of Early Christianity', *Method & Theory in the Study of Religion*, 23 3, pp. 238–56.

Vaage, Leif E., 1994, *Galilean Upstarts: Jesus's First Followers According to Q*, Valley Forge: Trinity Press.

———, 1995, 'Q and Cynicism: On Comparison and Social Identity', in Ronald A. Piper (ed.), *The Gospel Behind the Gospels: Current Studies on Q*, Leiden: Brill, pp. 199–230.

Walsh, Robyn Faith, 2021, *The Origins of Early Christian Literature: Contextualizing the New Testament within Greco-Roman Literary Culture*, Cambridge: Cambridge University Press.

Wright, Allen, 2023, 'Reconstructing Socio-Cultural Institutions in the Gospel of Mark', in Sarah E. Rollens and Patrick Hart (eds), *Worth More Than Many Sparrows: Essays in Honor of Willi Braun*, London: Equinox, pp. 200–19.

2

The Gospel of John

RODOLFO GALVAN ESTRADA III

The location of John's Gospel within the New Testament brings a fitting bookend to the portrayals of Jesus in the previous Synoptic Gospels (see Chapter 1). But how different is John's Gospel from the Synoptic Gospels? What are its unique contributions, background, and distinctions? These questions are key to ancient and modern understandings of the words of the Gospel of John. Therefore, this chapter begins by outlining the unique features of John's account of Jesus' life before moving on to highlight its distinctive theological themes. I then turn to an essential question for engagement with the Fourth Gospel: How has this Gospel been received and understood throughout history, up to the present day? To answer this question, the chapter will showcase differing ways that people have engaged with the text of John, from the early church through to modern biblical interpretation. Engaging with these varying approaches to the Gospel allows one to gain insights into the historical background, literary distinctiveness, and theological significance of John's Gospel, helping us to understand more fully why this Gospel has been impactful for Christian believers to the present day.

Overview

The Gospel of John is truly a distinct story of Jesus' life. The Gospel can be divided into sections that reflect the overall plot and pace of the story. There is a prologue (1.1–18); the public ministry of Jesus (1.19—12.50); Jesus' final words to his disciples (13.1—17.26); his final days, which includes the trial before Pontius Pilate and crucifixion (18.1—19.42); and several resurrection appearances (20.1—21.25).

When we compare John with the Synoptic Gospels, many notable differences arise. One will notice from the opening chapter that Jesus does not appear as a baby born in a manger as in Matthew. Nor do we find an immediate engagement in miracles of healing or spiritual battles with demonic powers as in the opening chapter of Mark. Also missing is the announcement of the Angel Gabriel to Mary about Jesus' birth, which is only found in Luke. John commences his Gospel at the beginning of all beginnings. The first words of the Gospel state, 'In the beginning was the Word, and the Word was with God, and the Word was God' (John 1.1). These first words draw the reader back to the creation story of Genesis 1—2, giving the reader the impression that the person who will be discussed in this Gospel is someone divine and from eternity.

Other scenes in John's Gospel are unique to his story. Most of the miracles in John are not found elsewhere. This includes turning water into wine at Cana (2.1–11), healing an official's son (4.46–54), healing a paralytic in Bethesda (5.1–15), healing a man born blind (9.1–12), raising Lazarus from the dead (11.1–45), and causing a post-resurrection miraculous catch of fish (21.4–11; see Luke 5.1–11). In fact, the only miracles John has in common with the Synoptic Gospels are the feeding of the 5,000 and Jesus' walking on water. Moreover, John describes the miracles of Jesus as 'signs' and not 'works of power', as commonly described in the Synoptics. In John, miracles lead one either to faith or to unbelief, depending on how one interprets the sign. In the Synoptic Gospels, faith is a prerequisite to receiving a miracle.

The early church tried to make sense of the differences between the Gospels but concluded that John's Gospel has a rightful place within the canon. In fact, Irenaeus explains that there can possibly be no more than four Gospels given that:

> There are four zones of the world in which we live, and four principal winds, while the Church is scattered throughout all the world, and the pillar and ground of the Church is the Gospel and the spirit of life; it is fitting that she should have four pillars, breathing out immortality on every side, and vivifying men afresh. (*Against Heresies*, 3.11.8)

Scholars today no longer adhere to a supplemental theory, that is, the belief that John was written to supplement the Synoptic Gospels. Instead, the Gospels were trying to lead people to faith and share the story of Jesus for their audiences. Overall, we can notice that both John and the Synoptic Gospels share a similar plot. Both include an appearance of John the Baptist, calling of disciples, miracles and healing, conflict with the religious authorities, cleansing of the temple, betrayal, arrest, trial, death, and resurrection. This demonstrates that John and the Synoptic Gospels shared a common tradition about Jesus. They both drew from a common source – the real events of Jesus – even though they were probably not dependent on each other.

Key themes

Who is Jesus?

John's portrait of Jesus, woven throughout the narrative, is made explicit in the concluding chapters. John states that 'these things', which includes all that Jesus did and said, 'have been written' so that the reader may believe that 'Jesus is the Messiah and Son of God' (20.31). Here we have a very direct statement for the readers. The Gospel's entire purpose ought to culminate in an understanding of Jesus as both the Messiah and Son of God. The Gospel thus far ought to help the readers continue in their faith, or come to faith for the first time, and have eternal life. How then does Jesus' identity as the Messiah and Son of God emerge throughout the Gospel? If anything, these two dynamics – sonship and messiahship – are not solely mentioned in these final chapters of the Gospel but woven throughout the entire narrative.

Jesus as Son of God

But first, what does it mean to be a 'Son of God'? Is this simply a divine claim, expression of kinship with God, or something else? This expression has a variety of meanings within the Old Testament. God calls Israel his 'son' and 'firstborn' (Ex. 4.22; Jer. 31.9; 4 Esd. 6.58; Pss. Sol. 18.4), and King David is God's 'firstborn' son (Ps. 89.27). It is believed that Israel as a people was personified as the only and unique son of God (Ps. 82.6), with the king also as the sole representative. To be a 'son of God' is thus a statement of peoplehood and kinship. It denotes the personal relation that Israel has with God as their Father. These expressions, however, become solely applied to Jesus in John's Gospel, which denotes his uniqueness.

Jesus' identity as the Son of God causes trouble with the religious leaders, who sought to kill Jesus because he was calling God his Father and claiming to be his Son (5.18). In John 5, Jesus reaffirms his identity by calling himself the 'Son of God' and offering life to anyone who hears his voice (5.25). A similar situation happens in another debate with religious leaders. This time, he is accused of blasphemy (10.33). The claim of being the Son of God is difficult for some religious leaders to hear (10.33–39).

To claim sonship, as they understood it, was to claim equality with God. This assertion is not taken lightly. In fact, during Jesus' trial they raise this issue with Pilate saying that according to their law anyone who claims to be the Son of God ought to be executed (19.7–9).

Only John's Gospel records Jesus as identifying himself as the 'Son of God'. This is not found on the lips of Jesus within the Synoptic Gospels. Overall, we can notice that religious leaders take Jesus' sonship claim seriously. It signalled Jesus' equality with God and power to grant life; not just eternal life but physical healing as well.

Jesus as Messiah

John also affirms Jesus' identity as Messiah. This term 'Messiah' specifically refers to the anointing of oil in special service to God. We find that priests, kings, and prophets were anointed for a specific task of service in the Old Testament.

The earliest mention of Jesus' identity as the Messiah comes from Andrew, one of John the Baptist's disciples. It is Andrew who tells his brother Peter that he had 'found the Messiah' when they become Jesus' followers (1.40–42). The Samaritan woman also anticipates the coming of the Messiah and tells Jesus that they are waiting for him to explain the meaning of Scripture (4.25). During this dialogue, and one of the few times within the Gospel, Jesus confesses his identity as the Messiah (v. 26).

At the end of Jesus' public ministry, the religious leaders tried to quash any growing faith in Jesus. Only John's Gospel mentions synagogue excommunication as a possible consequence for believing in Jesus' messianic identity (9.22). This, however, does not prevent other religious leaders from approaching Jesus and asking him directly to reveal whether he is the Messiah (10.24). Jesus responds to the public interest in his identity by pointing out that he has already revealed it and that his miracles should speak for themselves (vv. 25–26). Other Jewish people also question Jesus' identity when he starts talking about his coming death. The crowds even point out that the Messiah would live forever (12.34). Jesus, however, does not directly reply to their questions and leaves them in suspense.

Overall, Jesus' identity as the Messiah was debated by some but received by others. Jesus speaks publicly about his identity and even tells the religious leaders to look at the miracles as a witness to his identity. There is a hope that the readers would recognize that Jesus is truly the Messiah. Throughout the conversations, confrontations, and confessions, the readers may perhaps have their own doubts quelled and become convinced of Jesus' true identity. The Gospel ends with the recognition that everything that has been written aimed to convince them that Jesus was the Messiah and Son of God (20.31).

Reception: A history of reading John's Gospel

The Gospel of John has made a profound impact upon the history of the Church. This was the Gospel that helped resolve theological debates, form the creeds of Christian orthodoxy, and shape contemporary understandings of conversion with its 'born again' terminology, drawn from John 3. Indeed, the 'born again' description of conversion is so deeply embedded in American evangelical identity that it is almost another way of describing Americans who have some sense of fondness for Jesus. But John also has another history. The Gospel, in part, has been responsible for shaping a negative stereotype of Jews and has been examined as a colonial text. In this brief history of reception, I will review the impact of John not only upon the Christian tradition and theology, but also how it has been received and interpreted by feminist, Jewish, and postcolonial scholars. Also included are artworks of John during the medieval and Renaissance periods. This allows us to see how the text has resonated with a wide range of readers, each approaching the text from their own cultural situations.

Early readings of John

Traditionally, the Gospel of John has been understood to have been written by John the Apostle. Many early church fathers overwhelmingly affirm that the writer was John, one of Jesus' 12 disciples. In the second century, Irenaeus confirms that John the Apostle wrote the Gospel while he was staying in Ephesus. He states, 'John, the disciple of the Lord, who also had leaned upon His breast, did himself publish a Gospel during his residence at Ephesus in Asia' (*Against Heresies* 3.1.1). Irenaeus' testimony is not alone. Other early church fathers such as Tertullian (d.c. AD 220), Clement of Alexandria (d.c. AD 215), Dionysius of Alexandria (d.c. AD 265), and Jerome (d. AD 420) also affirm John the Apostle as author of the Gospel.

Although the early church testimony presents strong evidence for John's authorship, how reliable are these perspectives? Critical scholarship has taken a closer look at the Gospel itself and raised doubts. In fact, nowhere in the Gospel does the name 'John' appear in reference to the disciple.

Instead, the Gospel claims to be dependent upon 'one whom Jesus loved', also known as the 'Beloved Disciple'. Who is this mysterious person known as the Beloved Disciple? This person appears throughout the Gospel. For example, he is present when Jesus foretells his betrayal (John 13.23), stands at the foot of the cross (19.26), is with Peter at the tomb (20.2–10), fishes with Peter (21.7), and walks with Peter and Jesus along the sea (21.20–25). This is possibly the same unnamed disciple in 1.37–42 and the one who was with Peter in the courtyard of the high priest after Jesus was arrested in 18.15–16. Is the Beloved Disciple a symbolic figure, John the Apostle himself, or another person altogether? Perhaps scholarship has taken too much of a critical look at this unnamed figure. No other person from the 12 apostles seems to match this unnamed character except John the Apostle. And, traditionally, the early church fathers believed this to be so.

The Gospel may have first emerged in the late first century in the city of Ephesus. But we cannot be sure of the Gospel's provenance. Ephesus reflects various characteristics common to many Hellenistic cities, but we do know that according to early church tradition John the Apostle was known to have lived and been buried in this city (Eusebius, *Ecclesiastical History*, 5.24.3; Jerome, *On Illustrious Men*, 45). Church tradition has always associated the Gospel with Ephesus.

Another insight from Church tradition is the belief that John's Gospel was written after the Synoptics. Many Church fathers recognized the differences among the Gospels and tried to explain their relationship. Eusebius (d.c.340) and Jerome make mention that John's Gospel was written to supplement what was lacking in the earlier Gospels (Eusebius, *Ecclesiastical History*, 3.24.7; Jerome, *On Illustrious Men*, 9). Textually, we know that the Gospel could not have been written later than the second century. One of the oldest fragments of the New Testament is the John Rylands Manuscript (P[52]), which includes John 18.31–33 and 37–38. This manuscript is dated between AD 100–150. Its existence within the second century demonstrates that the Gospel was already circulated as far south as Egypt. Overall, the Gospel was known within one generation of the apostles and preserved by a community that relied upon the witness of John the Beloved Disciple. This leads us to conclude that the Gospel was written in the late first century between AD 60 and 100.

The context of the Gospel compels us to think about the circumstances related to emerging Christianity in the late first century. This was a period in which there was a gradual separation between Jews and Jewish Christians. Strikingly, this tension permeates the Gospel with its description of synagogue excommunication and portrayals of Jesus' experiences with his own Jewish people. The identity of the readers, also known as the Johannine community, has been vigorously debated in scholarship. Views range from those who believe that the primary readers were Gentiles to a much broader audience. Many now favour a broader or universal audience. Richard Bauckham writes in *The Testimony of the Beloved Disciple* (2007) that the 'author deliberately made his work accessible enough to outsiders for it to be read with profit by nonbelievers, Jewish or Gentile, who might be introduced to it by Christian friends' (p. 13). The proposition for a universal audience does not necessitate abandoning questions about the ethno-racial identity of the readers. A universal audience makes it even more necessary to pay close attention to the representation, portrayal, engagement, and manner in which the Jews, Samaritans, Greeks, and Romans emerge in the Gospel. One cannot fail to recognize that the Gospel itself has a special interest in detailing various ethnic groups who come into contact with Jesus. They too are part of the story because this story is also written for them.

In the second century, Clement of Alexandria described John as a 'spiritual Gospel' (Eusebius, *Ecclesiastical History*, 6.14.7). The Gospel, however, has not always been read and interpreted by Christians. It was the gnostic Heracleon who first published a commentary on John's Gospel around AD 170. Although we do not have copies of his commentary, fragments appear within Origen's *Commentary on the Gospel of John*, which was one of the earliest Christian interpretations of the Gospel. Origen's commentary not only interprets the Gospel for Christians but also seeks to refute false teachings that were appealing to 'inquisitive souls' (*Commentary on John*, 5.8). He interprets the Gospel on both the literal and spiritual level, often discussing only one level of interpretation and paying close attention to the language of the text, phraseology, or meaning found in related Old Testament texts. Although Origen never finished his commentary, he considered John as the 'first fruits of the Gospels', noting that no other Gospel manifests Jesus' 'divinity as fully as John' (*Commentary on John*, 1.22).

The early church certainly recognized the theological value of John's Gospel with its emphasis on Jesus' divinity. The Gospel helped Irenaeus in the second century combat false teachers, such as Valentinus, who were promoting gnostic ideas and the lack of Jesus' role in creating the universe (*Against Heresies*, 3.11.1–7). Then, in the fourth century, we find Athanasius' *Four Discourses Against Arius* utilizing the Gospel of John to argue for Jesus' divinity and relationship with God. A false teacher by the name of Arius was arguing that Jesus was a begotten creature and not fully divine. In response, Athanasius draws from various texts in John's Gospel that emphasize Jesus' divine identity to refute the notion that Jesus was a created being. He cites the Gospel's claims such as when Jesus states, 'The Father and I are one' (John 10.30) and 'I am in the Father and the Father is in me' (John 14.9–10). He also points to the Gospel where it asserts that 'all things came into being through him, and without him not one thing came into being' (John 1.3) and 'In the beginning was the Word' (John 1.1). As Athanasius argues, 'the Word of God is his Son, and the Son is the Father's Word and wisdom; and Word and wisdom is neither creature nor part of him whose Word he is, nor an offspring passibly begotten' (*Against the Arians*, 1.8.28).

John's Gospel formed the early Christians' understanding of Jesus' divine identity, his eternal pre-existence as the Word of God, and his role in saving humanity by becoming flesh. Without John's Gospel, Athanasius' theological rebuttal of Arianism would have taken another route, and perhaps even longer to understand and defend Christian trinitarian theology. It is noteworthy that the Nicene Creed (AD 325) and Constantinopolitan Creed (AD 381) describe Jesus as the 'only begotten Son of God' who was 'begotten' but 'not made'. The creed of Chalcedon (AD 451) also describes Jesus as the 'only begotten, God the Word'. Jesus' identity as the only begotten Son of God within these early creeds comes directly from John's Gospel.

Artistic receptions

While John's Gospel becomes a vital source for understanding Jesus' divine identity within Christian theology, not all receptions of John are found in literature. One of the earliest Christian paintings of Jesus depicts him as a shepherd, drawing on the Greco-Roman iconography of the *kriophoros* ('ram bearer'), but with a Christological significance as the Good Shepherd from John 10.11–18. These paintings are found in various catacombs of Rome dating from the second to the mid-third century. Possibly the earliest is Domitilla's catacomb which shows Jesus with a lamb on his shoulder, a staff in his left hand, and surrounded by various lambs. Another mid-second-century painting from the Catacomb of Priscilla in Rome portrays Jesus with a lamb on his shoulder with birds above him and lambs nearby his feet. Finally, the nearby St Callisto Catacomb, dated to the mid-third century, depicts Jesus carrying a lamb across his shoulder while holding a bucket. This portrayal of Jesus as a shepherd who carries sheep on his shoulder and draws sheep near him is deeply influenced by John's Gospel.

Early Christian art also associated the Gospel of John with one of the living creatures in Revelation 4.6–8. Irenaeus compares John to a lion, thus linking the Gospel with the 'effectual working, his leadership, and royal power' (*Against Heresies*, 3.11.8). But others, such as Bishop Victorinus of Pettau in the fourth century, associate John with the eagle. Victorinus comments, 'John the evangelist, like to an eagle hastening on uplifted wings to greater heights, argues about the Word of God' (*Commentary on Apocalypse*, 4.7). Likewise, Augustine also agrees and states, 'John, on the other hand, soars like an eagle above the clouds of human infirmity, and gazes upon the light of the unchangeable truth with those keenest and steadiest eyes of the heart' (*The Harmony of the Gospels*, 1.6.9). Since then, Christian art has associated the Apostle John and his Gospel with an eagle. For example, an early ninth-century ivory plaque from the Carolingian dynasty portrays John with a halo and an eagle above his head (The Metropolitan Museum of Art, 1977.421). He is sitting on a chair between two pillars with an open Gospel that has words in Latin, *In Principio Erat Verbum* (In the beginning was the word).

Along with the eagle symbolizing the Gospel, John is also depicted, in various compositions, as a young man. Most famously, Leonardo da Vinci's fifteenth-century painting of the Last Supper for the refectory of the Convent of Santa Maria delle Grazie, Milan, has John sitting on the right side of Jesus with fair skin, long hair, and no facial hair. Other fifteenth-century paintings depict John with a golden chalice, drawing back to a second-century apocryphal tradition when John survives a drink filled with poison. A young John holding a golden chalice is found in fifteenth-century artworks such as an engraving by German artist Israhel van Meckenem (c.1480–1500, The Cleveland Museum of Art, 1925.991) and as part of *The Donne Triptych* by Netherlandish artist Hans Memling (c.1478, The National Gallery, London, NG6275.3).

In sixteenth-century Spain, El Greco followed an established tradition, rendering a young John holding a poisoned golden chalice (c.1605, Museo del Prado, P002444; 1610–14, Museo del Greco, Toledo, CE00004). This youthful portrayal also appears in a 1793 painting by the French neoclassical painter François-André Vincent (Detroit Institute of Art, 80.6). He follows earlier iconographic traditions of John ready to write, portraying John as a beardless young man, with an eagle above his left shoulder, and his face lifted while writing (the artist's name!) in a book.

Fig 2.1 Unknown artist, Aachen, Germany, *Plaque with Saint John the Evangelist*, early ninth century, Elephant ivory, 18.3 x 9.4 x 0.7 cm, The Metropolitan Museum of Art, New York, The Cloisters Collection, 1977, 1977.421, courtesy of www.metmuseum.org.

Fig 2.2 Israhel van Meckenem, after Hans Holbein, *St John with Serpent in Chalice*, c.1480–1500, Engraving, The Cleveland Museum of Art, Gift of The Print Club of Cleveland 1925.991, Courtesy of The Cleveland Museum of Art.

Figure 2.3 François André Vincent, *Saint John the Evangelist*, 1793, Oil on canvas. Detroit Institute of Arts, Founders Society Purchase, Acquisitions Fund, 80.6., Courtesy of Detroit Institute of Arts.

This portrayal of John the Apostle as the youngest of all the disciples stems from the order in which he is mentioned in the Gospels. Since John is typically mentioned last, after his brother James, it is presumed that he was the youngest (Matt. 4.21; 10.2; Mark 1.19; 3.17; 10.35; Luke 5.10). His youthful age also helps explain why John was the last of all the disciples to have lived late into the first century.

Modern readings

While much art from the Renaissance portrays John as a young man, modern scholarship since the eighteenth century believed that the Gospel of John held little historical value for understanding the life of Jesus. Indeed, it was Adolf von Harnack's lecture at the University of Berlin in 1900 that most aptly reflected such a view. He states:

> the fourth Gospel, which does not emanate or profess to emanate from the apostle John, cannot be taken as an historical authority in the ordinary meaning of the word. The author of it acted with sovereign freedom, transposed events and put them in a strange light, drew up the discourses himself, and illustrated great thoughts by imaginary situations. (*What is Christianity?*, pp. 20–21)

Harnack viewed the Gospel of John as a creation of the writer. However, it must be noted that Harnack reflected the scholarship of the nineteenth century. Scholars such as F. C. Baur (1792–1860) and David Strauss (1808–74) also viewed John as too theological and thus historically unreliable. While more recent 'quests' to find the historical Jesus have primarily focused on the Synoptic Gospels, there has been another look at John's contribution to history and the historical Jesus. A recent Society of Biblical Literature series edited by Paul Anderson called *John, Jesus, and History* (2007–16) has attempted to recover John's contribution to our understanding of history and Jesus' identity. These volumes include the work of international scholars who are pushing back against the 'de-historicization of John' and 'de-Johannification of Jesus'.

While historical Jesus scholars dismissed John, it was Rudolf Bultmann in the 1940s and the ensuing scholarship of Robert Fortna which took an interest in the Gospel's composition and sources. This was during a time in which 'form criticism' was a prominent approach to studying the Gospels. Bultmann proposed a 'sign-source' theory, which argued that the evangelist drew from a source that contained a collection of miracle stories. This, he believed, was the foundational narrative that led to the eventual emergence of the Gospel as we have it today. Bultmann's 1952 commentary on John, in fact, reflects this attempt to understand the original chronological order of John. Following Bultmann, Fortna expanded this idea with an attempt to reconstruct the sign-source used by John. In his volume *The Gospel of Signs* (1970), Fortna claims that the Gospel itself has many aporias – that is, many inconsistencies – that cannot be accounted for, and this makes it difficult to determine where the text begins or ends. Like Bultmann, Fortna's sign-source sought to address the literary and theological tensions within the Gospel.

Although Bultmann and Fortna's sign-source theory shaped later discussion on the formation of John, not all were convinced. Other twentieth-century American scholars, such as Dwight Moody Smith and Raymond Brown, began to challenge the notion that the evangelist used a particular source for the Gospel. This was not the only view of Bultmann's that was discarded. Scholarship also rejected Bultmann's claim that the Gospel was greatly influenced by a gnostic Mandaeism tradition prominent in Syria around the second century. Since the discovery of the Dead Sea scrolls in Qumran (1947), scholarship on John has recognized that the Gospel's dualism and cosmology reflect Jewish views which were prominent during the first century.

While scholars debated the sources of John's Gospel, it was the monumental work of J. Louis Martyn's *History and Theology in the Fourth Gospel* (1968) that turned scholarship's attention to the community of the Beloved Disciple. Martyn proposed that the Gospel was written in the form of a two-level drama, intersecting between the Johannine community and their adversaries on one level, and the Gospel's depiction of Jesus and his opponents on another. The Gospel, in other words, witnesses both to the events during Jesus' lifetime, and also the actual events experienced by John's church. Martyn draws from a variety of texts, specifically the 'synagogue excommunication' language of the Gospel (John 9.22; 12.42; 16.2). Historically, Martyn claims that at some point prior to the Gospel there was an authoritative Jewish body in Jamnia that reached a formal decision outlawing public expressions of messianic faith in Jesus by mandating synagogue excommunication. Because this occurred at one historical level during the time of John's readers, the Gospel was composed in such a manner that reflects this experience. Other writers' works such as Brown's *Community of the Beloved Disciple* (1979) and John Ashton's *Understanding the Fourth Gospel* (1991; 2007) expand upon Martyn's hypothesis. They presume that the Gospel reflects possible ruptures and divisions between various Christians and Jewish believers. While very popular for some time, this view has taken much criticism and is no longer considered as a reasonable option for understanding the Gospel's background.

There were profound changes in the field of biblical scholarship with the emergence of new literary theories in the early 1980s, including the publication of R. Alan Culpepper's *Anatomy of the Fourth Gospel* (1983), Gail O'Day's *Revelation in the Fourth Gospel* (1986), and others who were reinterpreting the New Testament with the insights of literary criticism. They took up the challenge of looking at the final form of the Gospel in order to highlight those narrative dynamics that the traditional historical critical method had neglected. Certainly, Mark Allan Powell (1990) notices that while it may be an anachronistic approach for reading the Gospels, given that this method imposes on ancient literature concepts drawn from the study of modern literature, it has bridged the gap between scholar and layperson. These literary approaches, as Powell suggests, have brought scholars and non-professional Bible readers much closer together.

Overall, we can notice that scholarship on John has taken us into many directions. And while there has been recent discussion on where the new current of scholarship will take the direction of John's Gospel, for the remainder of this chapter I will focus on more recent attention given to the racial rhetoric of the Gospel in light of the Holocaust and postcolonial interpretations.

New currents

John's antisemitism, Jewish readings, and race

Throughout history, John's Gospel has unfortunately contributed to Jewish antisemitism with its harsh language and portrayal of the *Ioudaioi* (frequently translated as Jews) as the 'devil's children' (John 8.44). We can observe this in the writings and sermons of Martin Luther. While Luther was at first sympathetic to the Jews during his resistance to the Catholic Church, he became hostile in his writings later in his life. For example, Luther's sermon given on the fifth Sunday in Lent (1532) blurs the boundaries between the Jews as portrayed within John's Gospel and the Jewish people of his day. His sermon weaves the theological implications of the text with its impact upon Jewish–German Christian relations. Within his sermon, he argues that the Jews have no right to be called the children of God. He also penned a short letter called *Against the Sabbatarians* (1538) to demonstrate that the Jews have failed to receive Jesus as the Messiah and properly interpret the promises of the prophets. But it was his 1543 publication *On the Jews and Their Lies* that really put Luther's antisemitic views on full display. Here Luther advocates for the burning of synagogues, destruction of homes, confiscation of prayer books and Talmudic writings, death threats upon Jewish rabbis, travel bans, economic sanctions, and forced labour. If Christians do this, as he believes, they will honour God and Christianity. One of the most popular descriptions of the Jews that reverberates throughout Luther's writing is 'devilish', and it is this description that emerges from John's Gospel. Luther uses this language to argue that the Jewish people are no longer the people of God but have the devil as a father.

It must be noted that Luther's rhetoric planted the seeds of racial violence in Germany that later developed into more racialized and violent polemic against the Jews in the centuries to come. Yet, it was not until the aftermath of the Holocaust in 1945 that a reassessment of John's anti-Jewish language occurred among scholars. In the mid-sixties, scholars started to revisit their complicity and contribution to antisemitism. Jules Isaac raised this issue in 1964, and others, such as Rosemary Ruether in 1974, also made similar assertions. Then, in a 1975 article for *Journal of the Central Conference of American Rabbis*, Eldon Jay Epp admitted:

> The Fourth Gospel, more than any other book in the canonical body of Christian writings, is responsible for the frequent anti-Semitic expressions by Christians during the past eighteen or nineteen centuries, and particularly for the unfortunate and still existent characterization of the Jewish people by some Christians as 'Christ-killers'. (p. 35)

From 1998 to 2001, leading scholars met at the Katholieke Universiteit Leuven in Belgium to address the issue of 'John's antisemitism'. The results of these gatherings produced a scholarly response to and interpretation of John's Gospel from a variety of perspectives entitled *Anti-Judaism and the Fourth Gospel* (2001). Some contributors to this volume, such as James Dunn, tried to offer an alternative explanation to the harsh rhetoric of John's Gospel. He suggested that the polemic should be understood as an intra-Jewish polemic rather than anti-Jewish. But not all agree. The Jewish scholar, Adele Reinhartz, candidly states, 'My heart still sinks every time I open the Gospel of John to 8.44 and read that the Jews have the devil as their father' (2001, p. 167). In her book *Befriending the Beloved Disciple* (2001), she argues that the Gospel fosters an anti-Jewish attitude and sentiments with its binary choice in believing or rejecting Jesus' messianic claims and access to God. With regard to the Gospel's negative portrayal of the Jews and Judaism, Reinhartz insists in *Jesus, Judaism, and Christian Anti-Judaism* (2002), that 'any honest and engaged reading of the Gospel must surely acknowledge, and lament, the presence of these themes' (p. 114).

While John's Gospel presents Jesus as the Son of God and Saviour of the world, the worldview of the story only allows a binary option for the readers. This is what Reinhartz finds troubling. Although objections exist to admitting that the Gospel fosters anti-Jewish or antisemitic readings, it is difficult to explain away the negative portrayals and anti-Jewish senti-ments. Certainly, the Gospel of John contains positive portrayals of some Jewish characters. But racial rhetoric is not a zero-sum game. Positive portrayals in certain texts do not erase other harsh depictions. How we continue to read these texts as sacred Scripture while also recognizing that they are rooted in a specific and irretrievable context is the challenge we have as interpreters.

Postcolonial readings of John

A recent form of interpreting the Gospel of John is through the literary theory of postcolonialism. This literary theory has impacted multiple disciplines, not just biblical studies. According to R. S. Sugirtharajah in *Exploring Postcolonial Biblical Criticism* (2012), the origins of post-colonial literary theory did not begin in the academy but with the struggles of activist and creative writers who resisted imperial powers and colo-nial practices that oppressed indigenous people. This literary theory was also influenced by the monumental work of Edward Said. It was Said's *Orientalism*, published in 1978, that forever changed the way we under-stand how people-groups are represented in literature and academic discourse. Said's analysis of Western literature revealed that the European culture was defining itself in terms of cultural superiority by representing the Orient in an inferior manner. Said called into question the presumed objective portrayal of the 'other' within literature, reminding us that we cannot assume that portrayals are reality. While Said's theory has influ-enced a variety of fields and disciplines, biblical scholars have utilized his views to rethink how biblical texts have participated in colonial enter-prises, conquest of indigenous lands and representations of native people.

Postcolonial criticism has shaped the study of the New Testament with new hermeneutical insights and questions. One such scholar is Fernando Segovia with his 2009 commentary on John's Gospel that identifies the Gospel as a postcolonial text. Segovia lays out a grand outline of the Gospel's postcolonial vision by tracing how Jesus comes into conflict with the ruling circles of colonial power, which include the overseeing masters of imperial Rome. He remarks that the Gospel 'invalidates and displaces all existing institutions and authorities, values and norms, ideals and goals, while promoting and emplacing alternative' ones (p. 157). He traces through the plot of the Gospel and how Jesus clashes with colonial powers. In other words, the Gospel is not simply a story about Jesus' con-flict with spiritual or religious rulers. As Segovia remarks, it is a 'religious text with strong political overtones' (p. 164). This is not to suppose that the spiritual realm does not matter. It does. But the clash between Jesus and Satanic forces is one level of the multi-sided conflict. For example, since the prologue portrays the Word as revealer of God, this suggests that Rome and all other sanctioned worldly powers are deprived of their authority and delegation. Since Jesus is eventually killed by the political authorities, his death is understood as a 'clash of the kingdoms' (p. 189). As Segovia writes, the Gospel's 'postcolonial vision posits a reality-wide clash of kingdoms and empires' involving the 'kingdom of God' and the 'kingdom of Satan' (p. 189). Thus, on the one hand we can read John with attention to the conflict with spiritual Satanic forces, including its political representatives on earth and, on the other, the kingdom Jesus came to reveal, the other-worldly kingdom of God being made manifest on earth.

Reading the Gospel with this postcolonial perspective brings to the fore-front its political and imperial tones. Postcolonial scholars such as Segovia remind readers that John is situated in a colonial context of imperial Rome and calls them to be 'postcolonial' in that they too must continue Jesus' mission. This is done, as he explains, by being a 'colony' of God's Kingdom here on earth and resisting and 'raiding' the kingdom of Satan.

Other postcolonial scholars, such as Musa Dube and Jeffrey Staley in their volume *John and Postcolonialism* (2002), take a different approach and read the Gospel of John as a colonial tool. Dube and Staley note that the Gospel characterizes Jesus as one who comes from heaven to earth to assert power over space and time. As a text, it is also a site for struggle and power, prompting the reader to identify with Jesus, possess others, and displace their land. Their reading of John is most notable in their analysis of John 4. Here, Dube and Staley notice how this story of Jesus and the Samaritan serves to legitimize and authorize imperialism. How so? First, Jesus' statements to the disciples authorizes them 'to go, to enter, and to teach other nations' (vv. 37–38) articulates a search for profit and a desire to take possession. Second, the Samaritans are portrayed as people who 'require and beseech for domination' and the colonizers as people with a 'moral duty to the natives' (p. 65). This rhetoric authorizes the Christians 'to travel, enter, educate and to harvest other foreign lands for the Christian nations' (p. 65). And on a related theme, Dube insists that the teachings reflect the 'installation of Christianity as a universal religion' that 'relegate all other religions and culture to inadequacy' (p. 70). This analysis by Dube also stems from the context and experiences of her life as a Motswana woman of South Africa. Her reading for decolonization stems in part from an encounter with the New Testament functioning compatibly with colonialism.

Other scholars identify key Johannine themes and passages that empha-size the uniqueness and superiority of Jesus' identity over all religions and cultures. It is, however, important to recognize primarily that these readings aim to liberate the Gospel from the missionaries and evangelists who have historically weaponized John as a colonial tool of the empire. Whether or not the Gospel of John truly can be free from its colonial impulses is difficult to ascertain. As Sugirtharajah remarks, 'the Christian Bible, for all its sophisticated theological ideals like tolerance and com-passion, contains equally repressive and predatory elements which provide textual ammunition for spiritual and physical conquest' (2012, pp. 31–2). Nonetheless, postcolonial readings of John critically expose the use of the Gospel for colonial and culturally hegemonic purposes. However, it must be emphasized that the Gospel of John was not written for imperial inter-ests. It was written so that people may have the opportunity to receive eternal life through faith in Jesus (John 20.31). This also suggests that it is the responsibility of Christian believers always to ensure that the good news of John's Gospel remains good news for all people.

Recommended further reading

Brown, Raymond, 1979, *Community of the Beloved Disciple: The Life, Loves, and Hates of an Individual Church in New Testament Times*, New York: Paulist Press.
Carter, Warren, 2008, *John and Empire: Initial Explorations*, New York: T&T Clark.
Culpepper, Ray Alan, 1987, *Anatomy of the Fourth Gospel*, Philadelphia, PA: For-tress Press.
Martyn, J. Louis, 2003, *History and Theology in the Fourth Gospel*, Louisville, KY: Westminster John Knox Press.
Reinhartz, Adele, 2001, *Befriending the Beloved Disciple: A Jewish Reading of the Gospel of John*, New York: Continuum International.

References

Ashton, John, 2007 [1991], *Understanding the Fourth Gospel*, Oxford: Oxford University Press.
Bauckham, Richard, 2007, *The Testimony of the Beloved Disciple: Narrative, His-tory, and Theology in the Gospel of John*, Grand Rapids, MI: Baker Academic.
Baur, Ferdinand Christian, 1844, 'Ueber Die Composition Und Den Charakter Des Johanneïschen Evangeliums', *ThJb(T)*, 3: 1–191, 397–475, 615–700.
Bieringer, R., D. Pollefeyt, and F. Vandecasteele-Vanneuville (eds), 2001, 'Anti-Judaism and the Fourth Gospel: Papers of the Leuven Colloquium, 2000', in *Anti-Judaism and the Fourth Gospel*, Louisville, KY: Westminster John Knox Press.
Brown, Raymond E., 1966, *The Gospel According to John*, Garden City, NY: Doubleday.

————, 1979, *The Community of the Beloved Disciple*, New York: Paulist Press.

Bultmann, Rudolf, 1952, *Das Evangelium des Johannes. Ergänzungsheft*, Kritisch-exegetischer Kommentar über das Neue Testament, Göttingen: Vandenhoeck & Ruprecht.

Culpepper, R. Alan, 1983, *Anatomy of the Fourth Gospel: A Study in Literary Design*, Philadelphia, PA: Fortress Press.

Dube, Musa and Jeffrey Staley (eds), 2002, *John and Postcolonialism: Travel, Space, and Power*, London: Bloomsbury Publishing.

Epp, Eldon Jay, 1975, 'Anti-Semitism and the Popularity of the Fourth Gospel in Christianity', *Journal of the Central Conference of American Rabbis*, 22 4, pp. 35, 43, 45–52.

Fortna, Robert Tomson, 1970, *The Gospel of Signs: A Reconstruction of the Narrative Source Underlying the Fourth Gospel*, London: Cambridge University Press.

Harnack, Adolf, 1901, *What Is Christianity? Lectures Delivered In The University Of Berlin During The Winter Term 1899–1900*, trans. Thomas Bailey Saunders, New York: G.P. Putnam's Sons.

Heine, Ronald E., 1989, *Origen: Commentary on the Gospel According to John, Books 1–10*, Fathers of the Church, Washington, DC: Catholic University of America Press.

————, 1993, *Origen: Commentary on the Gospel According to John, Books 13–32*, Washington, DC: Catholic University America Press.

Lenker, John Nicholas (ed.), 2000, *Sermons of Martin Luther*, vol. 2, 7 vols, Grand Rapids, MI: Baker Academic.

Martyn, J. Louis, 1968, *History and Theology in the Fourth Gospel*, New York: Harper & Row.

O'Day, Gail R., 1986, *Revelation in the Fourth Gospel: Narrative Mode and Theological Claim*, Philadelphia, PA: Fortress Press.

Powell, Mark Allan, 1990, *What Is Narrative Criticism?*, Philadelphia, PA: Fortress Press.

Reinhartz, Adele, 2001, *Befriending the Beloved Disciple: A Jewish Reading of the Gospel of John*, London: Continuum.

————, 2002, 'The Gospel of John: How the "Jews" Became Part of the Plot', in Paula Fredriksen and Adele Reinhartz (eds), *Jesus, Judaism, and Christian Anti-Judaism: Rereading the New Testament after the Holocaust*, Louisville, KY: Westminster Press, pp. 99–116.

Said, Edward W., 1978, *Orientalism*, New York: Pantheon Books.

Schaff, Philip (ed.), 1888, *Saint Augustin: Sermon on the Mount, Harmony of the Gospels, Homilies on the Gospels*, A Select Library of the Nicene and Post-Nicene Fathers of the Christian Church, vol. 6, New York: Christian Literature Company.

Segovia, Fernando F., 2009, 'The Gospel of John', in R. S. Sugirtharajah and Fernando F. Segovia (eds), *A Postcolonial Commentary on the New Testament Writings*, London: T&T Clark, pp. 156–93.

Smith, Dwight Moody, 1995, *The Theology of the Gospel of John*, Cambridge: Cambridge University Press.

Strauss, David Friedrich, 1855, *The Life of Jesus, Critically Examined*, trans. by Marian Evans, New York: C. Blanchard.

Sugirtharajah, R. S., 2012, *Exploring Postcolonial Biblical Criticism: History, Method, Practice*, Chichester: Wiley-Blackwell.

Weinrich, William C., 2011, *Latin Commentaries on Revelation*, Downers Grove, IL: Inter-Varsity Press.

3

Acts of the Apostles

JAMES CROSSLEY

This chapter is about how we read and interpret the narrative of a biblical text. The focus is Acts of the Apostles (hereafter: Acts) which tells the history of the rise and spread of the Christian movement, roughly from the aftermath of Jesus' death (c. AD 30) to the AD 60s. Acts is the second volume following the first – Luke's Gospel (see Luke 1.1–4; Acts 1.1) – and together they are known as 'Luke–Acts'. They make up nearly a quarter of the New Testament.

When reading these documents, as this chapter will show, it is helpful to take both together to help us understand the agendas in Acts, including key themes of the Spirit-fuelled spread of the message, attitudes to possessions, and movement from Jerusalem to Rome. It will also show that while the connection between Luke and Acts is clear enough, scholars provide conflicting suggestions when trying to establish who wrote (Luke–)Acts, when, and for whom.

This chapter further provides a close narrative reading of Acts in order to delve deeper into one of the central issues of modern Acts scholarship: understanding the new Christian movement in relation to Jews and Judaism. Acts 11.26 may be the earliest known use of the label 'Christians', and it appears after the main advocate of Gentile inclusion, Saul/Paul, has joined the movement (Acts 9) and after Peter has a vision which justified the increasing inclusion of Gentiles (Acts 10). The chapter will show how this inclusion of Gentiles and (to some degree) non-observance of Jewish Law (the commandments based on Genesis–Deuteronomy) are two of the most important intertwined issues in Acts, with significant ramifications for the text's presentation of Jews and Judaism. This close reading is designed to draw out differing interpretations and understandings which have arisen regarding these most important issues, while also seeking to locate the text in its theological and social contexts.

The final part of the chapter explores the ramifications of readings of Acts in lived experience, particularly in European politics, including imaginings of new social orders in England in the 1300s, Shakespearean

43

post-Reformation reservations, and late twentieth-century Socialism. This allows us to see how the discussions above had ongoing influences and continue to present challenges to this day.

Overview

We begin with a summary of the text of Acts. And here we face the first problem. What is 'the text'? There were two differing forms of Acts in the early church known (among other things) as the Alexandrian text and the Western text. The Alexandrian text is shorter and typically regarded as closer to the earliest or 'original' versions of Acts and usually represented in English translations, as it (largely) will here. Nevertheless, when we approach Acts, it is important to bear in mind that we are not necessarily reading the same version as many readers before us.

Acts opens by addressing 'Theophilus', referring to the previous book about Jesus' life, death, resurrection and ascension to heaven (1.1–11). Jesus ordered the apostles to stay in Jerusalem where they would receive the Holy Spirit and then spread the message far beyond. On the day of Pentecost, they are filled with the Holy Spirit and given the ability to speak in different languages (Acts 2). Peter explains to the crowd that this is a fulfilment of prophecy, and that Jesus was the promised Messiah. Therefore, the Jewish crowd should repent, get baptized and receive the Holy Spirit; around 3,000 join the movement.

The first believers share all their goods in common, although some hold possessions back and are struck dead (Acts 5). Led by Peter and John, they spend time in the Temple at Jerusalem, carry out healings, wow the onlookers, eat together and preach about the risen Messiah. Peter and John are arrested and released, arrested again by Herod, and freed by an angel as the Temple authorities are unsure what to make of it all (Acts 4—12).

As the movement continues to grow, Stephen works signs and wonders. He is arrested, gives a potted 'biblical' history from Abraham to Solomon's building of the Temple and, finally, Spirit-filled, sees a heavenly vision as he is stoned to death (Acts 6—7). Enter Saul, who is involved in the persecution of the Jerusalem church (8.1–3). However, this only further enables the spread of the message, with Philip successful in Samaria and beyond (8.4–40).

While on the road from Jerusalem to Damascus, Saul has a vision, as does a puzzled disciple who is told that Saul has been chosen to spread the word to Gentiles, kings, and the people of Israel. Saul is baptized, flees a plot to kill him in Damascus, and visits a frightened Jerusalem church (Acts 9).

Peter also has a vision, proclaiming he may do what he has never done before: eat foods prohibited to Jews. On meeting a centurion named Cornelius, who was told by an angel to send for Peter, the ramifications of this vision become clearer: Gentiles can now repent and receive the Holy Spirit and baptism (Acts 10—11). The inclusion of Gentiles causes debates including which Jewish practices should be kept, with the movement eventually deciding that Gentiles turning to God did not have to uphold the whole of the Law (Acts 15).

Saul and Barnabas travel to Cyprus, beginning more extensive Mediterranean travels for Saul, now (usually) Paul (Saul is his Aramaic/Hebrew name; Paul is his Greek name). They gain Jewish followers but turn to proclaiming the message to Gentiles (Acts 13—14). After separating, Paul travels westward to Macedonia, Thessalonica, Athens, and Corinth, and a familiar pattern ensues: debates with Jews and Gentiles, successful conversion, persecution, and continuation (Acts 16—20).

Finally, heading towards Jerusalem, Paul realizes that imprisonment and persecution await him. He makes a public display of upholding specific laws but is seized by Jews from Asia who accuse him of defiling the Temple with Gentiles. As opponents try to kill him, Paul is arrested (Acts 20—21). After appealing to have the emperor's tribunal, he travels to Rome, via a shipwreck on Malta, and the book concludes with Paul living under guard, able to preach unhindered to visitors for two years (Acts 28).

Key themes

Beginning in Jerusalem ... and Luke's Gospel

The Gospel of Luke prepares the theological geography of Acts through Jerusalem (compare Luke 24.6–7 with Mark 16.1–8; Matt. 28.7–10) to Rome. Ideas relating to the growth and spread of the movement are present at the beginning of Jesus' ministry according to Luke. In Jesus' inaugural teaching in the synagogue at Nazareth – which, unlike Matthew and Mark, is placed at the beginning of Jesus' public activities (Luke 4.14–30; see Mark 6.1–6; Matt. 13.54–58) – Luke stresses the importance of the Holy Spirit and Scripture, providing a divine justification for the movement centred on Jesus that would be unstoppable in its growth (Luke 4.14, 17–21, 30). The divine authorization of the progression of the message through the Spirit and scriptural fulfilment is tied in with Luke's emphasis on Jesus' remarkably long (in narrative terms) and inevitable journey to Jerusalem (Luke 9.51—19.27).

At the end of the Gospel, the resurrected Jesus emphasizes the importance of Jerusalem, setting the scene for Acts: the Messiah had to suffer and be raised from the dead and now 'repentance and forgiveness of sins is to be proclaimed in his name to all nations, beginning from Jerusalem' (Luke 24.44–47). In Acts, as we have seen, the message then spreads from Jerusalem throughout the Mediterranean, the Roman Empire, and beyond (see Acts 8.26–40), until it culminates with Paul – the hero of much of Luke's second volume – preaching in Rome and unstoppably so despite being under house arrest (28.23–30).

Major themes and theology can be read as grounded in this geographical movement, including those anticipated in Luke and taken up in Acts, such as the Messiah, repentance, the inexorable spread of the movement and the role of the Holy Spirit as a kind of parallel to the Roman Empire (for more on the geographical movement, see Nasrallah, 2008).

The Holy Spirit

Acts opens by explaining that Jesus was taken up to heaven after 'giving instructions through the Holy Spirit to the apostles whom he had chosen' (1.2). Therefore, the Holy Spirit is an especially common theme in Acts and interconnected with the spread of the movement, regularly accompanied by miracles and overcoming setbacks. The Spirit becomes associated with Paul in his spread of the message (see Acts 19.6), including the authorizing of his journey to Rome (see Acts 19.21).

The Spirit is integral to marking out membership and discipline of the early community. In Acts 2, the Spirit is poured out on the believers who are then able to speak a range of languages. This enabled the spread of the message to thousands more and further miracles. Also, the Spirit sets apart Paul and Barnabas for the work of spreading the message (Acts 13).

After the outpouring of the Spirit, the apostles inspire awe as they preach before authorities and perform signs and wonders including raising the dead (Acts 9.36–43; 20.7-12), miraculously disappearing (Acts 8.39–40), and having power over serpents (Acts 28.1–6). Furthermore, the apostles, as well as Ananias and Paul, are enabled to impart the Spirit to believers through the laying on of hands (see Acts 8.17–19; 9.17; 19.6; see Deut. 34.9).

Money

In Acts, there are the beginnings of an idealized community where believers shared all things in common (Acts 2.44–46; Acts 4). This is grounded in ideas associated with Jesus in Luke's Gospel (Luke 16; 18.18–30). Acts 5 makes clear how serious the theme of money in relation to the Spirit is to this understanding of the early community when Ananias and Sapphira keep back some of the proceeds of a property they sell. This withholding of the proceeds is deemed a lie against the Holy Spirit and thus God, and they are struck dead (5.1–11). It is a sign of the importance of this idealized way of living that means Ananias and Sapphira die because of their actions (see Davies, 2008; also Chrysostom, *Homilies on the Acts of the Apostles*, 12).

This clear distinction between the power of the Spirit and the wrong use of money is also made clear in Acts 8, where a man called Simon encounters the power imparted by the apostles by the laying on of hands. Simon, who has a reputation for performing signs, offers money so that he may receive the ability to impart this power. He is met with a stiff rebuke from Peter: 'May your silver perish with you, because you thought you could obtain God's gift with money! You have no part or share in this, for your heart is not right before God' (8.20–21).

Reception

Scholarly reader debates: Author, date, location

Despite this lengthy narrative and its prominence in the New Testament canon, there are many uncertainties about the origins of Acts, as we have already seen with the variant texts. Given that Acts has sections written in the first-person plural ('we': Acts 16.10–17; 20.5–15; 21.1–18; 27.1–37; 28.1–16), readers have naturally speculated about the identity of the author and when were these various events brought together into what became known as 'Acts of the Apostles'.

Even the title is not without its difficulties. 'Acts of the Apostles' seems to have been known by the late second century, thanks to a reference in Irenaeus' *Against Heresies* (3.13.3), though how much earlier this title was used we cannot say.

The author does not provide their name in the text of Luke–Acts nor is there a direct indication of the ethnicity of the author – we do not know whether they come from a Jewish or non-Jewish background. This has led to some guesswork in identifying the author and the kind of background readers should assume to be behind this document.

It is possible someone called Luke with a close connection to Paul wrote Luke and Acts, based on the 'we' sections and Colossians 4.14 ('Luke, the beloved physician ... greet[s] you'). Certainly, the view that this person was called Luke, that he was a physician, and that he was a companion of Paul was the dominant assumption in the later Christian church (see Irenaeus, *Against Heresies*, 3.1.1, 3.14.1; Tertullian, *Against Marcion*, 4.2.2; Clement of Alexandria, *The Stromata*, 5.12.82; Jerome, *On Illustrious Men*, 7; Eusebius, *Church History*, 6.25.14; Muratorian Canon).

However, there are significant counter arguments. It is regularly argued by modern scholarly readers that the 'we' passages were more of a literary convention than direct evidence for eyewitness testimony. A further suggestion is that the figure of Luke might have been seen as a convenient figure for later Christians to provide textual authority precisely because he was associated with Paul (for example, Philemon 1.23–24; Col. 4.10–14; 2 Tim. 4.11). In another standard literary convention of the time, so this argument goes, Lukan authorship was 'falsely' added at some point (see Chapters 5 and 7 for more on pseudepigraphy).

Scholarly readers have looked for clues in the text of Luke–Acts to see if there are indications of historical events or cultural tendencies that hint at the date of its composition. For example, the narrative ends in the AD 60s with Paul under arrest in Rome and so Acts must have been written after that. Luke–Acts has typically been dated to after the fall of Jerusalem to the Romans in AD 70 (see Luke 19.41–44; 21.20–24), sometimes generally in the late first century. However, there has been an increasingly influential scholarly trend to push the dating of Acts into the second century (see, for example, Tyson, 2006). Even so, challenges to these dates have not disappeared and Jonathan Bernier's 2022 volume *Rethinking the Dates of the New Testament* has again raised the possibility of Acts being written shortly after the events narrated about Paul in Rome in the 60s. Readerly consensus remains elusive.

Place of writing is not easy to establish because of a lack of early evidence. Often using Jerome's fourth-century suggestions, guesses have included Antioch, Achaia, and Rome. One of the reasons given for a later dating is that Acts has similarities with (and some argue, dependency upon) the works of the first-century Jewish historian Josephus, who wrote a defence of Jewish practices. Irrespective of whether a close relationship exists, a comparison can be instructive as both present a history of, and apology for, their respective group and interests.

For instance, a common argument is that Acts presents the origins of the 'Christians' as a group to show that they should not be seen as a threat to imperial order, even if they were sometimes associated with disturbances. In *Acts of Empire* (2020), Christina Petterson goes one step further. She argues that the narrative of Acts is uncritically embedded in some of the major assumptions, structures, and ideology of the Roman Empire, from acceptance of slavery through the replication of received gender roles in the Roman patriarchy to the economic dominance of cities where much of the action in Acts takes place. This too can be seen as part of Acts functioning as an apology for the reasonableness and social acceptability of the new Christian movement.

Reading with social context: First called Christians (Acts 11.26)

From Judaism...

We now come to what has been a central issue for modern scholarly readers: the complicated question of Acts' understanding of the new Christian movement in relation to Jews and Judaism. These questions become central to readers because we live in a post-Holocaust world facing up to the disturbing legacies of Christian anti-Judaism and nineteenth-century understandings of Jews in relation to ideas of race and the nation state.

As stated above, the Spirit in Acts legitimizes the inclusion of Gentiles in the spread of this movement that began among Jews and for Jews (for example, 10.44–46). This has led to a range of answers to questions about the attitude towards Jews in Acts, with views ranging from claims that the text is philosemitic through ambivalent to antisemitic (for a summary of the discussion see Moraff, 2020). How the author of Acts might have self-identified in relation to Jews and Judaism or identified the Christians in relation to Jews and Judaism may not be entirely clear – nor indeed how a range of outsiders might have viewed this relationship as presented in the narrative. Therefore, a close reading of Acts allows us to see how we can approach the text while hearing the (often conflicting) scholarly views about this topic.

What is clear is that Luke presents the movement as starting out as a Jewish movement with Jesus and beginning in Jerusalem. And then, through a kind of revelation history (see Acts 9—10), this narrative is constructed in terms of unravelling how the Jewish Law was or was not to be observed in relation to increasing numbers of Gentiles in the movement. While critics cannot (or at least should not) insist what makes someone a Jew or not (views varied in the ancient world anyway), some prominent ancient observers of early Judaism (for example, Juvenal, *Satires*, 14:96–106; Tacitus, *Histories* V), and those who identified as Jews (Judith 12.7–19; Tobit 1.11; 1 Macc. 1.11–15; *Letter of Aristeas*, 180–81; Josephus, *Jewish Antiquities*, 20.34–48), did note certain flashpoints over Jewish identity, such as Jewish Law generally, Sabbath observance, food laws, eating habits, circumcision of male infants and sometimes adults, and worship of a distinctive god.

These are some of the assumptions shared in Luke–Acts, or at least there is an assumption that understanding the relationship between the movement and Jewish Law was crucial for understanding Jewish–Gentile relations. Luke's Gospel certainly has plenty of controversies between Jesus and his opponents, but these are not presented as a generalized Jewish opposition in the way we sometimes see in John (see Chapter 2) and in Acts.

Crucial to understanding Acts is something missing from Luke's Gospel. In what is sometimes labelled the 'Great Omission', Luke leaves out Mark 6.45—8.26 which could have been understood (even if wrongly) as support for overriding the food laws (see Mark 7.19) and the beginning of Gentile inclusion inaugurated in Jesus' lifetime (see for example, Mark 7.26–31; 8.1–11). This cannot be the case for Luke's Gospel because the same author in Acts is emphatic in claiming that these issues first occurred some time after Jesus' death and provides divine authority for this claim in the story of Peter's vision (10—11.18).

Stephen, Hellenists, and Saul

So, Peter's vision marks a departure from the early movement when it was active in and around the Jerusalem Temple – or does it? Acts certainly presents the martyrdom of Stephen (Acts 6—7) in connection with allegations of Stephen speaking blasphemously against the Law but Acts claims these are false witnesses (6.11–14). It is sometimes argued that Stephen is presented as speaking against the very idea of a material Temple and a sacrificial system outlined in the Law, with reference to Acts 7.45–50. This is a view with a long reception history, stretching back centuries. For instance, the famed English monk and ecclesiastical historian Bede (AD 672/3–735) argued that Stephen claimed that God 'does not place a high value on dressed stone but rather desires the splendour of heavenly souls' and that the Temple would have to be destroyed 'when a better dispensation came to take its place' (*Commentary on Acts of the Apostles*, 7.44).

The reading of Stephen's words as an attack on a material Temple has endured but it has been challenged. Translation plays a part in these debates. English translations sometimes render Acts 7.47 as 'But it was Solomon who built a house for him'. This sounds like a strong contrast with what came before. However, the Greek (*de*) here is much weaker than the English 'but' and can be translated with 'and' or not translated at all. This would mean that the description of Solomon building the Temple is a simple continuation of the story described in the Old Testament/Hebrew Bible. This might be expected, given that Stephen otherwise appears to accept the validity of the 'biblical' history of Israel and the story of Moses and the giving of the Law (for example, 7.20, 22, 38, 53). Stephen's real criticism is found in Acts 7.48: 'Yet the Most High does not dwell in houses made by human hands.'

Stephen's comments do not, then, have to be read as a criticism of the biblical past. As Peter Doble (2000) argued, these comments are another endorsement of the biblical ideas about where God does and does not dwell and the importance of keeping the commandments under threat of the destruction of the Temple (1 Kings 8; 2 Chron. 6; Ps. 132; Isa. 66.1–2). Moreover, Acts is picking up on the idea that a place 'made with hands', a term associated with idolatry, is the problem. Instead, Acts presents Stephen as arguing that the Temple has become idolatrous and its guardians have failed to interpret the Law properly and so the inevitable consequence is that the Temple will be destroyed (6.14; see Luke 13.34–35; 19.39–46; 21.20–24). Stephen's opponents naturally disagree with this assessment and have him killed.

Even so, some traditional Protestant scholars, such as the influential Martin Hengel (1983), have argued that from this story we can deduce that Stephen belonged to a subgroup of Greek-speakers called 'Hellenists'. They opposed the very existence of a Temple and sacrificial system, rejected some parts of the Law, and were opposed by Aramaic-speaking believers called 'Hebrews' (6.1–6). Whatever the historical realities behind the text, this is certainly not how Acts presents the *dispute* between the two groups. Instead, the presentation in Acts is consistent with the central feature of this early idealized community, namely the correct distribution of resources: 'the Hellenists complained against the Hebrews because their widows were being neglected in the daily distribution of food' (6.1). Indeed, once resolved this dispute led to the movement inevitably spreading, including among priests from the Temple no less (6.7).

Similarly, among such traditional Protestant scholarship can be found the argument that Saul's conversion or call (9.1–19; 26.12–18; Gal. 1.15–17) effectively brought about (for Saul/Paul at least) the idea that the Law was no longer necessary in the face of grace (for more see Kim, 1981). Again, whatever the historical realities behind the text, this is not how Acts presents the story. Like the earliest believers of Acts 1—5, Saul finds himself in disputes after his change of allegiance, but Acts does not claim that this is about the Law. In the case of Saul according to Acts, we get some straightforward explanations: he was considered a traitor by his former associates (9.20–23) and treated with deadly suspicion by some of his new colleagues among the 'Hellenists' who had previously been persecuted by Saul's circle (9.29; see also 9.13–14). Obviously, before his change of allegiance, Saul was understood as having his reasons to persecute the earliest followers of Jesus (8.1–3) and presumably these reasons involved something like what we discussed in the case of Stephen ('And Saul approved of their killing him', 8.1).

But what of the reasons for attacking Paul, according to Acts, when the opposition in Damascus, from which he has to flee, is generalized as Jewish (9.19–25; cf. 2 Cor. 11.30–33)? For Acts, it seems that the reasons for the controversy involved claiming Jesus was the Son of God and the Messiah. Why might this have been understood as a problem? It could be, of course, that Acts wants to root its theology in disagreement with, and differentiation from, Jews and Judaism.

That may or may not be the case, but it seems likely that we are meant to envision Saul's preaching as disrupting the ways in which Jewish groups had established their worship practices in multi-ethnic settings and as a threat to the wellbeing of the Jewish community in an urban centre, an issue that recurs in Acts (see 17.1–15). Paula Fredriksen contextualized such thinking in relation to Christian origins in *Paul: The Pagan's Apostle* (2017). From the perspective of Acts, the fears that Christianity is an unfairly disruptive movement must be allayed, and it is instead the argumentative and rhetorical abilities of Saul/Paul that were dismissed by his opponents. Throughout the narrative, and despite (or because of) Jewish supporters of the movement, Acts regularly presents a near-generalized Jewish opposition as ultimately mistaken and unreasonable, but which cannot stop the inevitability of the spread of Christianity.

The end of the Law of Moses?

Acts presents the question of the Law in connection to Jewish–Gentile relations in Peter's vision and its interpretation (10—11.18). Until this point, Acts has assumed that the Law had been part of the movement's everyday life, so Peter explains that he has never eaten food prohibited in the Law when commanded to kill and eat. However, now there is a definitive judgement to the contrary: 'What God has made clean, you must not call profane' (10.15; 11.9). This is the clearest indication that, for Acts, the food laws are now no longer in force for both Jews and Gentiles in the movement. Unsurprisingly, the Christian interpretation of this passage could focus more precisely on the famous specific example of prohibition of eating pigs (for example, Cyril of Alexandria, *Against Julian*, 9.318–19).

Acts further shows how this vision must be interpreted in light of inclusion of Gentiles in the movement which, as ever, gets further authorization from the Holy Spirit (10.45). Peter claims: 'You yourselves know that it is unlawful for a Jew to associate with or to visit a Gentile; but God has shown me that I should not call anyone profane or unclean' (10.28). This is a curious claim because it is not technically accurate – there were a range of opinions among Jews about interactions with Gentiles, from table fellowship to social distancing. However, the claim that Jews did not interact or eat with Gentiles was a known stereotype held by some non-Jewish writers in the ancient world (for example, Diodorus, *Bibliographa Historica*, 34.1.2; Philostratus, *Life of Apollonius*, 5.33). Presumably, the author of Acts was employing this anti-Jewish stereotype to heighten the claim that Gentiles were now to be part of the movement and that at least some famous parts of the Law involving eating regulations were no longer in force.

Peter's vision thus marks a turning point in the story of Luke–Acts and the spread of the movement. In Acts 13.38–39, Paul is now presented as preaching that the Law is not fully required:

> Let it be known to you therefore, my brothers, that through this man forgiveness of sins is proclaimed to you; by this Jesus everyone who believes is set free from all those sins from which you could not be freed by the Law of Moses.

The role of the Law of Moses according to the Paul of Acts has puzzled commentators, although there have been plenty of solutions offered. According to the ancient Christian interpreter Ammonius, the Law of

Moses was not unjust but it was difficult and could only justify 'those who had followed the entire law perfectly'. This meant that the Law was incapable of justifying people because 'one who had fallen into a single crime was made guilty of all' (*Catena on the Acts of the Apostles*, 13.39).

Whether Acts 13.38–39 tallies precisely with the presentation of the Law in Paul's letters is another question (see Chapter 4). According to one of the most influential modern interpreters of Acts, Hans Conzelmann, there is 'only a slight hint of Pauline teaching' here, adding that, for Acts, the Law of Moses was 'an intolerable burden … which is thoroughly un-Pauline' (1960, p. 160). However persuasive Conzelmann's reading may or may not be, it was made as part of an important larger claim about the structure of Luke–Acts.

Conzelmann argued that Luke–Acts establishes a redemptive history whereby the period of Jesus' ministry and the period of the church are two different but overlapping epochs, with the epoch of Israel understood as prior to the period of Jesus' ministry. Within this understanding, the Law prepares the way for the Gospel as Israel does for the church and its mission. The period when the Law and Temple mattered for Christians no longer mattered in the present and was a part of the church's unrepeatable past, though legacies of that past continued. The earliest community in Acts (including Paul) kept the Law of Moses, and the meeting over the problem of the Law in Acts 15 is resolved in an 'ecclesiastical regulation' which maintains continuity with this past while delineating two phases of the church's history (1960, pp. 13–17, 160–61).

While the specifics of Conzelmann's arguments are for another time, in terms of the narrative, Acts 13 clearly indicates that something has now changed significantly in terms of Law observance, setting the scene for the resolution in Acts 15. It is also notable that Paul is preaching to both a Jewish audience and Gentiles sympathetic to Jewish ideas (13.26) which may again imply that the Law has changed for *both* Jews and Gentiles as in Acts 10—11.18. Indeed, this looks like another turning point for Acts as a generalized Jewish opposition are enraged on the following Sabbath while Paul and Barnabas claim that Jewish rejection has prompted the turn to the Gentiles instead, all of which is again endorsed by the Holy Spirit (13.44–52).

How literally do we take Acts here in this generalizing of Jewish opposition? Do we follow Jack T. Sanders in *The Jews in Luke–Acts* (1987) and make a case for Luke–Acts as an anti-Jewish text? As with Luke's use of the stereotype about supposed Jewish non-association with Gentiles, this might be another exaggeration to make the point about Gentile inclusion, perhaps reflecting the reality of the audience for Acts (assuming it was largely Gentile). Of course, this does not mean people from Jewish backgrounds can no longer be part of the movement. After all, Paul and Barnabas were Jewish, and Paul goes out of his way to stress his heritage (21.37–22.3). Acts 15 is especially important in this respect because it shows the difficulties surrounding the acceptance or non-acceptance of parts of the Law for a movement that has been shown to spread among Gentiles, including mention of (the obviously Jewish) Pharisees who were also believers (15.5).

Acts 15 notes that there were certain figures who insisted that circumcision for Gentile men was necessary for salvation, in contrast to the views of Paul and Barnabas. This led to a meeting in Jerusalem with the main figures of the movement (and more Gentile converts en route). Peter recalled his role – with authorization from the Holy Spirit – in the justification for Gentile inclusion in relation to the Law. James framed the discussion in terms of Gentiles turning to God and that guidance was needed for them. A decision is therefore made that a letter should go out to Gentiles asking them to abstain from things sacrificed to idols, sexual immorality, blood, and (depending on which manuscript of Acts is used) that which has been strangled (Acts 15.20, 29).

Whatever the precise meaning of these prohibitions, they look like they are based on the commandments given to Noah in Genesis 9.3–17 which were understood to apply to all humanity:

> Only you shall not eat flesh with its life, that is, its blood. For your own lifeblood I will surely require a reckoning: from every animal I will require it and from human beings, each one for the blood of another, I will require a reckoning for human life. Whoever sheds the blood of a human, by a human shall that person's blood be shed. (vv. 4–6)

Understanding the regulations of Acts 15.20, 29 poses some difficulties for interpreters, and discussions are technical. But there is another general problem perhaps less difficult to resolve. If these are the restrictions placed on Gentile believers, does that mean behaviours are otherwise unrestricted? Clearly this was not typically the case in Christian thinking (cf. Gal. 5) and some, such as Origen (d.c. AD 253), sought to spell this out with reference to Acts 15.20, 29. The Holy Spirit, he argued, directs believers and 'since other crimes are avenged by laws of the world, it seemed superfluous for those things, which are sufficiently covered by human law, also to have been forbidden by divine law' (*Commentary on Romans*, 9.28).

Resolving tensions

Note that in Acts 15 the rules are primarily aimed at Gentiles not being required to observe parts of the Law, whereas some passages prior to Acts 15 appear to suggest that this reasoning applies to both Jews and Gentiles. While Acts does not fully explain this apparent tension, one explanation is that the role of the Law *in salvation* might be downplayed for both Jew and Gentile (13.44–52) but the habit of *practising* the Law might nonetheless continue among those who have practised it all their lives (most likely, but not exclusively, Jews). This is akin to Paul's reasoning in Romans 14.5–6:

> Some judge one day to be better than another, while others judge all days to be alike. Let all be fully convinced in their own minds. Those who observe the day, observe it in honour of the Lord. Also those who eat, eat in honour of the Lord, since they give thanks to God; while those who abstain, abstain in honour of the Lord and give thanks to God.

Despite Peter's vision in Acts 10—11.18, it is perhaps significant that Jews are not explicitly presented as eating pork or the like in Acts, and nor are they anywhere in the New Testament texts. This may reflect certain social realities: no matter what certain Jewish followers of Jesus theorized about the function of the Law in relation to Christ and salvation, eating pork or giving up lifelong practices did not necessarily follow. It is striking that in Acts, Paul had Timothy (son of a Jewish woman and believer and a Gentile man) circumcised on his missionary travels because of the presence of Jews in a certain region. From the perspective of Acts, this may be due to pragmatic reasons and cultural expectations so that the message can spread with less hindrance (quite how Timothy felt about this, we are not told), though it is still possible that Acts did not present Paul as believing that the commandment for male Jews to be circumcised should be overridden in any circumstance.

Indeed, Acts is aware of how the complexities of the observance of the Law and the spread of Christianity contributed to major misunderstandings. Acts can, therefore, be seen as a defence of Paul's views against misunderstandings. When Paul visits believers in Jerusalem (Acts 21), he is informed that Jewish believers have been told that 'you teach all the Jews living among the Gentiles to forsake Moses, and that you tell them not to circumcise their children or observe the customs' (v. 21). To alleviate the situation, they agree to what seems like another pragmatic solution: Paul is to undergo a vow and purification from the Law (see Numbers 6) so that they will see that the rumours about Paul promoting a hard anti-nomian attitude among Jews are false. In the meantime, the letter from the Jerusalem meeting in Acts 15 would show the sort of prohibitions in place for believing Gentiles.

The plan may not have been successful, and the ensuing misunderstanding may have led to Paul's arrest, but it gives some further insight into the logic of the role of the Law and its social ramifications in Acts.

That the uneasy reasoning in Acts about the role of the Law is likely akin to Paul's irenic reasoning in Romans 14.5–6 and its similarities to the pragmatism of 1 Corinthians 9.20–21 is telling. Paul is hardly without his polemical side in Romans, but he is not as aggressive as he was earlier in Galatians, where he went as far as wishing for his opponents to castrate themselves (5.12). Acts, however, is representing the more conciliatory version of Paul. We know that the realities of the debates over Law observance and Gentile inclusion were much more controversial than Acts portrays, at least if Paul's letters are anything to go by, including his account of a meeting in Jerusalem and an argument in its aftermath at Antioch between Peter and Paul and perhaps even James (Gal. 2.1–15). This would support the common claim in scholarship that Acts is a myth of Christian origins that downplays significant strife and disagreements, possibly trying to unify different tendencies within the movement, particularly when it comes to the leading heroic figures such as Peter, James, and Paul. The presentation of the Law in Acts attempts to unify all three.

We have talked about pivotal movements in Acts but Acts 15 is arguably *the* pivotal moment. It is a chapter that adds to God and the Holy Spirit further authority for the spreading movement, namely bringing Peter, James, and Paul together in a united front, as an alternative to a presentation of them in other contexts that foregrounds potential disagreements (see Gal. 2.11–15). Once there is an agreement on how to justify the inclusion of Gentile believers, Paul is then freed up to continue his epic travels spreading the message – if regularly misunderstood – around the eastern Mediterranean that may have reminded readers or hearers of the famous *Odyssey* by Homer. Moreover, it is a misunderstanding of the Law and the very agreement in Acts 15 that culminates in Paul's arrest and the spread of the movement to the heart of the Empire: Rome.

Acts, then, is not antisemitic or anti-Jewish in the sense of hating Jews as a distinct racial or ethnic group. Rather, Jews and Judaism serve as a foil for Acts to present and justify the new Christian group and this involved religious and ethnic generalizations which can be uncomfortable for the modern reader, even if they were common enough in the ancient world.

Having read carefully through Acts, we can see that it presents Christian origins as a movement that emerged from Judaism and Jewish believers into a movement with increasing numbers of Gentiles. It justifies this development as a kind of revelation history whereby the big changes away from famous Jewish practices centred on the Law were authorized through a divine vision, the Holy Spirit, and the leading human authorities. While there are presentations of a generalized Jewish opposition to this portrayal of Christian origins in Acts, it is aware of Jewish involvement in the movement and tries to explain something of Jewish concerns and interests. Nevertheless, it is a text partly designed to explain and authorize a movement that was looking increasingly like a Gentile one, and Jews remain a convenient foil for Act's apology for the innocence and reasonableness of the Christian movement.

Clunky generalizations about differences from Jews and Judaism can be explained as part of the original contexts for the writing of Acts and its justification for a movement that emerged out of Judaism, and has its roots in Judaism, but was beginning to identify itself as something distinct from Judaism as stereotypically understood in the ancient world and constructed by the author of Acts. The text was obviously written before the long history of Christian anti-Judaism and European antisemitism. Nevertheless, some of the emphases of Acts fed into the near inevitable notions of Christian superiority over a rival religion.

Ramifications of reading Acts

Lived experience

Such assumptions of theological superiority are at work, for instance, in Cyril of Alexandria's fifth-century anxious assessment of Peter's vision. Cyril also claimed that 'while holy Peter still desired to follow the customs of the Jews, and since he was trying to advance towards better things', he was 'terribly overcome by his reverence for these figures', and so Peter's reluctance is explained in terms of speaking 'as a Jew'. It took a rebuke from God for Peter to understand 'that the time had come when the shadows had to be transformed into truth' (*Against Julian*, 9.318–19).

These assumptions about the downgrading of Judaism are part of the problem with Acts: generalizing comments about Jews can be appropriated for anti-Jewish and antisemitic agendas, including in institutions and movements wielding power and influence. This has, of course, been the fate of influential and deadly receptions of the New Testament right up to the modern era, including Nazi Germany, as Susannah Heschel has shown in *The Aryan Jesus: Christian Theologians and the Bible in Nazi Germany* (2008).

The influence of the narrative of Acts has had an impact on the history of interpretation in other ways. In the modern era of critical scholarship, there may be more scepticism towards including miracles and the Holy Spirit in critical historical reconstructions and explanations of Christian origins, but paraphrases of the story of great men spreading the message through the eastern Mediterranean beginning from Jerusalem and getting to Rome still dominates. In other words, the scholarly pursuit of 'Christian origins' is often still based on the narrative model provided by Acts. This tradition had a landmark publication this century in James D. G. Dunn's monumental book from 2008, tellingly entitled *Beginning from Jerusalem*. Such scholarship has been done at the expense of alternative social historical approaches to Christian origins which might look at the importance of networks, trade routes, ancient modes of production, long-term socio-economic causes, and so on, for explaining the eventual emergence of Christian origins. There have, however, been challenges to this model, such as class- and material-based understandings as Robert Myles and I argue in the final chapter of *Jesus: A Life in Class Conflict* (2023). These also include the interdisciplinary, anthropologically oriented, collaborative work of the Redescribing Christian Origins group associated with the Society of Biblical Literature in North America.

Yet, the model of idealized origins also has a long reception history of challenging institutionalized models of authority. Over the centuries, numerous marginal, apocalyptic, millenarian, and countercultural movements have used the model of ideal origins in Acts to criticize a given authoritative church for failing to live up to expectations – and not least the failure to share things in common and distribute according to need which took on nationwide significance in Christian countries.

To give an example of how the community with things shared in common can be read in contrasting ways and according to a given agenda, we can look at an example of a narrow time and place: England in the 1370s and 1380s. The theologian and philosopher John Wycliffe reflected on the early church and Acts and theorized that if everyone ought to be in a state of grace and lords of the world, then all God's goods ought to be in common (*De civili dominio* 1.14; see also 3.77–81). This thinking which permitted the idea that those deemed righteous held legitimate authority, and those in mortal sin did not, could be a useful argument in high political battles with the church and ecclesiastical figures deemed sinful, such as for aristocratic figures using such anticlerical ideas to counter ecclesiastical power.

A reformist text from around this time, William Langland's dream vision *Piers Plowman*, was concerned about friars going to the universities, learning about philosophy, and making bold claims about how all things ought to be in common (*Piers Plowman* B.20.276). Also, around the same time, the English Peasants' Revolt took a different line, arguing that England needed dramatic transformation and the end of serfdom, exploitation, and domination by the lords and leading clergy in order to bring about a time when all things will be shared in common. This likely involved a stripping back and redistribution of church wealth among the laity and peasant access to game in rivers, parks, and woods (see Jean Froissart, *Chroniques*, 10.96; *Anonimalle Chronicle*, 137–138; Henry Knighton, *Chronicle*, 218–219).

Unsurprisingly, then, declarations of all things in common continued to create fear among those with a vested interest in maintaining the received order. In Reformation England, such ideas could be seen as an indicator of a group like the Anabaptists taking Reformation ideas to a wild and dangerous extreme. Shakespeare played on these established anxieties in *Henry VI, Part II*, where the megalomaniacal rebel leader Jack Cade's version of all things in common involved murder of the elites, female sexuality let loose, and drunkenness (*2 Henry VI* 4.7.8–9, 15–20, 63–67, 120–25).

Nevertheless, all things in common was still taken up as part of a more serious alternative hope for the future by religious groups which was later transformed into political aspirations and appropriated for more secularized agendas. Towards the end of the twentieth century, the radical English politician Tony Benn (1925–2014) tried to bridge what he saw as religious and secular traditions with reference to the early chapters of Acts and their applicability for public ownership of resources. In a 1995 talk in Sheffield, UK, he opposed the drive towards privatization of industry, claiming that anyone who thinks 'common ownership was invented by Karl Marx … might go back to the Acts of the Apostles for the idea of all things in common.'

Such is the dominance of the narrative of Acts, at least in Western imaginations: it can justify dominant political and theological ideologies but, in presenting an idealized view of the origins of the movement, has simultaneously bequeathed a narrative constantly holding such ideologies to account and pointing to the possibility of an alternative world beyond them. The history of interpretation shows that it certainly can be read in such ways. Whether the writer of Acts would have approved is yet another question.

Recommended further reading

Alexander, Loveday, 2007, *Acts in its Ancient Literary Context*, London: T&T Clark.

Conzelman, Hans, 1960, *The Theology of St. Luke*, London: Faber and Faber.

Davies, Douglas J., 2004, 'Purity, Spirit, and Reciprocity in the Acts of the Apostles', in Louise J. Lawrence and Mario. I. Aguilar (eds), *Anthropology and Biblical Studies*, Leiden: Deo Publishing, pp. 259–80.

Moraff, Jason F., 2020, 'Recent Trends in the Study of Jews and Judaism in Luke–Acts', *Currents in Biblical Research* 19 1, pp. 64–87.

Petterson, Christina, 2020, *Acts of Empire: The Acts of the Apostles and Imperial Ideology*, Eugene, OR: Cascade Books.

References

Benn, Tony, 1995, 'The Power of the Bible Today', *Sheffield Academic Press Occasional Papers: The Twelfth Annual Sheffield Academic Press Lecture, University of Sheffield, March 17, 1995*, Sheffield: Sheffield Academic Press, pp. 1–13.

Bernier, Jonathan, 2022, *Rethinking the Dates of the New Testament: The Evidence for Early Composition*, Grand Rapids, MI: Baker Academic.

Burrow, John and Thorlac Turville-Petre (eds), 2014, *The Piers Plowman Electronic Archive, Vol. 9: The B-Version Archetype*, Society for Early English and Norse Electronic Texts, available at http://piers.chass.ncsu.edu/texts/Bx.

Crossley, James and Robert Myles, 2023, *Jesus: A Life in Class Conflict*, London: Zero Books.

Doble, Peter, 2000, 'Something Greater than Solomon: An Approach to Stephen's Speech', in Steve Moyise (eds), *The Old Testament in the New Testament: Essays in Honour of J. L. North*, Sheffield: Sheffield Academic Press, pp. 181–207.

Dobson, R. B. (ed.), 1983, *The Peasants' Revolt of 1381*, New York: Palgrave Macmillan.

Dunn, James D. G., 2008, *Beginning from Jerusalem: Volume 2, Christianity in the Making*, Grand Rapids, MI: Eerdmans.

Fredriksen, Paula, 2017, *Paul: The Pagan's Apostle*, New Haven, CT: Yale University Press.

Hengel, Martin, 1983, *Between Jesus and Paul: Studies in the Earliest History of Christianity*, London: SCM Press.

Heschel, Susannah, 2008, *The Aryan Jesus: Christian Theologians and the Bible in Nazi Germany*, Princeton, NJ: Princeton University Press.

Kim, Seyoon, 1981, *The Origin of Paul's Gospel*, Grand Rapids, MI: Eerdmans.

Martin, Francis (ed.), 2006, *Acts*, Ancient Christian Commentary on Scripture: New Testament 5, Downers Grove, IL: InterVarsity Press.

Nasrallah, Laura, 2008, 'The Acts of the Apostles, Greek Cities, and Hadrian's Panhellenion', *Journal of Biblical Literature* 127 3, pp. 533–66.

Poole, Reginald Lane, Johann Loserth, and F. D. Matthew (eds), 1885–1904, *Iohannis Wycliffe Tractatus de civili dominio*, 4 vols, London: Wyclif Society.

Sanders, Jack T., 1987, *The Jews in Luke–Acts*, London: SCM Press.

Tyson, Joseph B., 2006, *Marcion and Luke–Acts: A Defining Struggle*, Columbia, SC: University of South Carolina Press.

Warren, Roger (ed.), 2003, *Henry VI, Part Two*, Oxford: Oxford University Press.

4

The Pauline Epistles, or An Introduction to Letters from the Gentile Mission

ISAAC T. SOON

In the anthology of the New Testament, there are 13 letters attributed to Paul the Apostle, one of the most prominent Jewish itinerants in the early Jesus movement. Paul was a Jewish teacher born outside the land of Judea (he was a Diaspora Jew, possibly with Roman citizenship) who lived around the middle of the first century AD.

To call the 13 letters in the New Testament 'Pauline Literature' is to obscure what was really a collective and collaborative enterprise between Paul and his co-workers like Timothy (2 Cor. 1.1; Phil. 1.1; Col. 1.1; 1 Thess. 1.1; 2 Thess. 1.1), Silvanus (1 Thess. 1.1; 2 Thess. 1.1), Sosthenes (1 Cor. 1.1), a secretary like Tertius (Rom. 16.22), and letter carriers such as Phoebe (Rom. 16.1–3) and Tychicus (Eph. 6.21–22; Col. 4.7; Titus 3.12; 2 Tim. 4.12). In Galatians, Paul even includes 'all the members of God's family' as epistolary senders (Gal. 1.2). We should really be talking about 'Letters of the Gentile Mission', since their composition involved numerous personnel, all focused on non-Jewish churches throughout the ancient Mediterranean world. In this chapter, I emphasize authors named in the letter openings, but readers should note that work is being done to problematize the inaccurate portrayal of Pauline letters as primarily 'authored' by only Paul himself; an idea that masks the collaborative but also enslaved situations that produced 'Paul's letters' (see Moss, 2023).

The titles of the letters were likely assigned by scribes as they were transmitted by early communities. Each title designates a community within a particular geographic destination: the city of Rome, the city of Corinth, and so on; or individuals, such as Timothy and Philemon. The inclusion of numerals (for example, 1 Corinthians, 1 Timothy) designates multiple correspondences to the same addressees. Although such titles give the impression of intentional order, there are some letters that may be composite assemblies of letter fragments (2 Corinthians, Philippians). They also remind readers that Paul's letters are not exhaustive treatises but specific communiqués to specific communities and individuals.

Out of all other texts in the New Testament, it is perhaps these letters that generate the lion's share of scholarly writing, usually under the banner of 'Pauline Studies'. The reader should find comfort in the fact that while an introductory chapter such as this could never be exhaustive, there is no one expert in Paul who even comes close to a comprehensive understanding of the increasing literature each year. The risk with Pauline scholarship is that we only 'see in a mirror dimly' (1 Cor. 13.12). Still, although Paul himself cannot be tamed, the writing under his name can be understood. As we shall see in this chapter (and the next), the corpus ascribed to Paul helps us to understand the multiple influences on this body of letters, and thus showcase the multifaceted writing process that makes up the New Testament. We shall also see how the figure connected to each letter, Paul the Man, has been created, and the contemporary scholarly work that is being done to question the concepts enamelled into this figure.

Overview of the Letters

The following provides general outlines of the letters in canonical order. An overview such as this is not a substitute for a thorough and slow reading through of Paul's letters (in multiple translations and in the ancient languages where possible). Readers should take the outlines here as provisional, especially given that some letters (such as 2 Corinthians and perhaps Philippians) may be composite.

Romans

Paul with Tertius (16.22) writes to the Roman assemblies in order to prepare them for his arrival at Rome and then through to Spain (1.11–15; 15.14–33). In many ways, the letter concerns core aspects of the Gentile mission and Paul's particular gospel. The authors argue that all humanity, both Jew and non-Jew, must deal with sin in light of the impending final judgement where everyone will be judged on their works (1.16—2.16; 3.1–20). A particular warning is given to those who call themselves Jewish (possibly Gentile proselytes to Judaism) who observe circumcision but who neglect other matters of the Jewish law (2.17–29). The Jewish law is important for revealing what sin is but does not itself have the power to remove sin from the human person permanently, something only trust in Christ can remedy for both Jew and non-Jew (3.21–31; 5—6). Abraham (the patriarch from Genesis 12—24) is the ultimate example of how this trust functions (4.1–25). This new life through Christ and the Holy Spirit reshapes the believer's relationship with the Jewish law (Rom. 7—8). Paul also reveals the necessity of his ministry for ethnic Jews of Israel (Rom. 9—11). Paul then turns to community and wider social ethics (Rom. 12—15.12). He closes by drawing attention to his large network of fellow workers both locally and abroad (Rom. 16).

1 Corinthians

This letter from Sosthenes and Paul from Ephesus (16.8) to the assembly in Corinth (a city on the isthmus between the Peloponnese peninsula and the rest of Greece) deals with numerous issues that have arisen after Paul's initial ministry there including: factionalism (1.10–17; 3.1—4.21); irregular sexual practices like incest (5.1–13; 6.12–20); and internal litigation (6.1–11). Paul also instructs the Corinthians on sexual conduct in marriage, singleness, and divorce (7.1–16, 25–40) as well as food offered to idols, and their relationship to demonic powers (8.1–13; 10.1—11.1). He also defends his apostleship (9.1–27), an issue that becomes an increasing concern in the following letters. The latter part of the letter concerns issues of worship such as whether women should cover their heads (11.2–16), the administration of the Eucharist (the Lord's Supper; 11.17–34), spiritual practices and speaking in multiple languages (12.1–31; 14.1–25), love (13.1–13), and orderly worship (14.26–40). Finally, Paul ends with a full explanation of the resurrection of the dead, its mechanics, and its connection to the death and life of Jesus (15.1–58). He reminds the Corinthians of the monetary collection for Jerusalem (16.1–4) and his present travel plans (16.5–12).

2 Corinthians

Timothy and Paul follow up with the Corinthian congregation, presumably after a second visit (13.1–2). This letter emphasizes the present sufferings of the authors (1.3–11), an explanation for why Paul has not returned to Corinth again (1.12—2.4), and his current ministry struggles in Troas and Macedonia (2.12–17). He was worried that his ministry in Corinth had been in vain (2 Cor. 7). Numerous times in the letter Paul details the specific suffering he has endured (2 Cor. 6; 11—12), and he spends a large amount of time explaining both the legitimacy of his own apostleship and competency through God despite his ministry being characterized by death, suffering, and the destruction of his body (2 Cor. 3—5; 10—13). This contextualization of his ministry within the frame of paradoxical strength in weakness is meant to instruct and transform the Corinthian perception of following Christ (12.19–21). Paul also continues to instruct the congregation about the monetary collection to Jerusalem (2 Cor. 8—9).

Galatians

Paul writes to communities in Galatia (Asia Minor) because some of them appear to be taking on Jewish circumcision, contrary to the initial gospel that Paul preached (1.6-10). He provides autobiographical information about his life in Judaism, the apocalyptic revelations he had of Jesus, and his mission to the Gentiles (1.11—2.10). Of particular importance is a confrontation with the Apostle Peter where Gentiles are compelled to observe Jewish customs, and Jewish believers refuse to eat with non-Jews (2.11–14). Paul is insistent that both Gentiles and Jews are made right to the God of Israel through the faithfulness of Jesus, not through works of the law like circumcision (2.15–21; 5.2–15; 6.11–15). Key to Paul's message is Abraham, Abraham's wives Hagar and Sarah (4.21—5.1), and the inheritance of their children which now has been made available to non-Jews through Jesus (3.1-29). Since believers now live by the Spirit, they do not need circumcision to facilitate godly living (5.16–26).

Ephesians

Paul writes from prison (3.1; 4.1) to a community in Asia Minor. Some of our ancient manuscripts lack Ephesus as the intended city and some early Christians thought it was addressed to Laodicea (see Col. 4.16). The letter is sent by Tychicus (6.21). Paul praises Jesus Christ for his work in uniting believers through adoption to a divine inheritance, the removal of sin, and the future glory marked by the Holy Spirit (1.3–14). Even though he has never met them, Paul prays vigorously for them (1.15–23; 3.14–21). Paul's prayer also substitutes as a way of conveying his gospel message: that Jesus was raised from the dead through God's power and was made the highest authority in all creation (1.20–23). Christ has made believers alive from being dead in sin and raises them by grace through faith for good works (2.1–10). Paul addresses specifically how the non-Jewish community has been brought into a single community (a holy temple, 2.21; a household, 2.19) by Christ's blood, making peace between Jews and non-Jews and, also, non-Jews and the God of Israel (2.11–22). He also explains his unique role to the non-Jews in the Mediterranean and connects his own personal suffering for the benefit of believing communities in Asia Minor (3.1–13). Calling for unity among the community, Paul calls them to work together in whatever role they play in the 'body' of Christ (4.1–16), including as wives, husbands, children, parents, enslaved persons, and enslavers in Christ-believing households (5.21—6.9). He encourages them to abandon their previous pagan ways of living (4.17—5.20). The letter finishes with a visually striking portrayal of godly military armour that believers require against cosmic powers of darkness (6.10–20).

Philippians

Timothy and Paul write to the believers in Philippi and address specifically the bishops and deacons of the community (1.1). Paul writes from prison, still managing to find opportunities to preach Christ even though opponents are trying to thwart his plans (1.12–18). Paul reflects on the bodily cost of his ministry to the nations and that he would much rather die and be with Christ but remains living for the sake of communities like those at Philippi (1.19–26). Through one of Paul's fellow workers, Epaphroditus, the Philippians have sent provisions to Paul to relieve him in prison (2.19–30; 4.10–20). One of the issues that Paul addresses may be disunity and a conflict between two congregational women leaders, Syntyche and Euodia (2.1–5; 4.2–3). An alternative reading is that these women are the bishops and Paul is merely reminding the Philippian community to be of one mind with them. Paul uses Jesus' humiliating example to illustrate service over exaltation (2.5–18). He also warns the community against people who might use their status to boast in themselves (3.1–6). Instead, Paul encourages the Philippians to imitate him by counting anything that might be a benefit to him as a loss to gain Christ (3.7—4.1).

Colossians

A letter from Timothy and Paul to the community in Colossae whom they have not yet personally met (2.2), but who have heard the gospel through a fellow worker named Epaphras (1.3–8) who has reported back. Timothy and Paul focus on the identity of Jesus above creation, cosmic powers and the church (1.15–18), as well as the saving work of Jesus through his death on the cross (1.19–23). Paul then speaks directly to the Colossians about his specific mission to the nations to make known the mystery of Christ and to nurture mature followers of Christ (1.23–29). Colossae and the neighbouring city of Laodicea are a part of Paul's mission to reveal God's knowledge of Jesus (2.1–5). Paul is particularly concerned that the Colossians live holy lives (3.5–10, 12–17) but also that they are not 'taken captive' by teaching that is different from Paul's own message about Christ (2.8–23). Like Galatians, Paul stresses how being clothed with a new self figuratively breaks down ethnic and social divisions (3.11). Paul then turns to right behaviour in the household, addressing wives, husbands, children, enslaved persons and enslavers (3.20—4.1). Paul has sent the letter from prison (4.10, 18) with his co-worker Tychicus and Onesimus (4.7–9), the latter who appears to be returning to Philemon his enslaver.

1 Thessalonians

A letter from Silvanus, Timothy, and Paul to the assembly in the city of Thessalonica. They recount the community's initial encounter with the gospel in both word and power, and how even through persecution the assembly became a resounding example to all Macedonia and Achaea (1.2–10; 2.13–15; 3.3–4). The three authors recount their suffering at Philippi and their intimate manner of ministering to the community, like a nursing mother and caring father parenting their own children (2.1–8, 11–12). They accepted no money from the community but worked themselves (2.9–10). Paul sent Timothy to check on the Thessalonians amid local persecutions and he reports that they have continued to stand firm (3.1–13). The authors then remind the community to continue living in a way pleasing to God, avoiding irregular sexual behaviour (4.1–8). They then briefly explain the mechanics of Jesus' return from heaven (4.13–18), although they emphasize that while the time of this return is unknown, vigilance is required (5.1–11).

2 Thessalonians

Silvanus, Timothy, and Paul continue their correspondence with the Thessalonian assembly amid their present persecutions (1.4–5; 2.13–17). In addition to comforting the Thessalonians who have become alarmed at how quickly Jesus might return (2.1–2), this time, the authors focus on the judgement of the Lord upon the earth (1.6–12) and of 'the lawless one' (2.3–12). Apparently, some of the Thessalonians have stopped working due to news of Jesus' impending return, a group the authors quickly rebuke (3.6–15). The letter is also concerned with correspondences circulating under Paul's name which have not been written by him (2 Thess. 2.2; 3.17).

1 Timothy

The first of four letters Paul addresses to individuals; 1 Timothy is addressed to Paul's closest companion, Timothy, whom he calls his 'child' (1.2, 18; see also 4.14). Timothy has been instructed to stay in Ephesus (the west coast of Asia Minor, modern-day Turkey) as Paul travels to Macedonia (1.3). Timothy's task is to instruct would-be teachers who are preoccupied with 'myths and endless genealogies' (1.4, 18–20) but who do not yet have proper understanding about what they are talking about (1.7). Paul argues that 'the law' (presumably the Jewish law) conforms to his own gospel entrusted to him (1.8–11). He then gives instructions about the 'household of God' (3.15), especially on appropriate prayers and worship and study (2.1–8), the treatment and distribution of community funds to young women and widows (5.1–16), and the behaviour of enslaved members of the community (6.1–2). He is particularly concerned with the way women dress and worship and how they should study in silence (2.9–15). Paul then lays out requirements for the offices of bishop and deacon (3.1–13) and the treatment of elders (5.17–22). Paul also opposes teachers who are inspired by demons and spirits (4.1), who prohibit marriage and abstaining from foods (4.3).

2 Timothy

This other letter to Timothy gives information about his family, particularly his grandmother and mother, Lois and Eunice (1.5). Paul apparently writes from prison in Rome (1.8, 17), where he has been abandoned by his co-workers in Asia (1.15) except for the household of Onesiphorus. He exhorts Timothy about his gospel and encourages him to hold to the standard of ideas that he has heard from him (1.13; 2.14–26; 4.1–5), of which the 'holy writings' can be a guide (3.15–17). Paul then speaks about how his suffering and endurance for the gospel is for the sake of 'the chosen ones' (2.8–13). He warns of teachers who are encircled by vices (3.1–9), who corrupt the truth that they teach. Paul, aware that his death is near (4.6–8), charges Timothy to imitate not only his teaching but his whole life (3.10–11), even to the point of persecution.

Titus

Paul writes to one of his co-workers named Titus (mentioned also in Gal. 2.3) from Nicopolis (on the west coast of Greece; 3.12) whom he left in Crete to appoint elders in every city in the region (1.5). Like 1 Timothy, Paul prescribes criteria for elders and bishops (1.5–9). Paul forcefully opposes dissenting teachers whom he calls 'those from the circumcision' (1.10), presumably Jewish Jesus followers (see also 'Jewish myths' in 1.14 and other controversies and legal disputes in 3.9). He encourages Titus to do the same (1.13–16). Paul emphasizes 'healthy teaching' (2.1) that is concerned more with ethical and virtuous behaviour among men and women, young and old (2.2–8), and enslaved persons to their enslavers (2.9–10) than points of doctrine. Jesus' saving work, where it does appear, is the catalyst for good behaviour and good works (2.14—3.8).

Philemon

This is the last of Paul's letters to an individual. Paul writes from prison (v. 23) to Philemon on behalf of an enslaved person named Onesimus (v. 10; see also Col. 4.9). Paul's specific request to Philemon, however, is ambiguous. It is unclear if Onesimus is a runaway enslaved person (a view from an enslaver's perspective) that Paul wants to manumit or if he wishes Philemon to transfer ownership of Onesimus to him. In either case, Paul exhorts Philemon no longer to view Onesimus as enslaved (v. 16) and states that any debt that he has incurred should be reckoned to Paul (v. 18).

Key themes

The implications of Jesus as Messiah

Central to these letters is Jesus of Nazareth as the Jewish Messiah. Although it undergirds all of Paul's discussions, Jesus' messiahship is not the primary focus of discussion. Rather, the letters focus on the implications of Jesus' messiahship for non-Jewish/Gentile and Jewish followers. Any benefits followers gain from Christ depends on trust in the divine gift of Jesus' death and resurrection (for example, Rom. 3.21–26; Gal 2.15–21). When followers are baptized in water under Jesus' name, they are baptized into his death where their sinful part of their humanity dies (for example, Rom. 6.3–11). What replaces that sinful flesh is the Holy Spirit that enables even Gentile believers to obey God's commands and laws without being inhibited by sin. Pledging allegiance to Jesus as Messiah has ethical and social effects, especially for non-Jewish believers. Their individual, sexual, ritual, and household behaviours must all now align to Jewish ethics and scriptures (for example, Eph. 5.21—6.9). At the same time, these non-Jews are to remain Gentiles and not try to become Jewish by circumcision (for example, Gal. 5.2–6). The Holy Spirit not only has a present effect but a future one as well. Having died with Christ, followers can anticipate being raised with him in the future resurrection of their bodies. Resurrection is not mere body resuscitation, but a transformation into an astral or supra-cosmic material (for example, 1 Cor. 15.35–49).

Weakness in strength

Where Jesus' messiahship does become a focus in the letters, it is in the pervasive theme of weakness in strength. The victory of a crucified messiah is both scandal and paradox, which has shaped Paul's own early Christian mission. Paul and the apostles experience physical hardship, as imitators of Jesus' own weakness (for example, 1 Cor. 4.9–13; 2 Cor. 6.4–5; 11.23—12.10). Yet they are to view this weakness as strength. This defies the logic and wisdom known among non-Jewish communities and causes problems for figures like Paul, whose apostleship and authority come under scrutiny. In general, the letters favour a communal ethic geared towards 'the weaker', the person who is most likely to stumble based on another believer's behaviour (for example, eating idol meat, see Romans 14.1–4). Submission to established authorities, men, husbands, and masters, is reinforced, and the community as a whole is characterized by fraternity, as all believers become children of Abraham and the inheritance promised to him by the God of Israel (see Gal. 3.29).

Enslavement

The letters also emphasize the former enslavement of believers to sin and their new enslavement to the God of Israel. Liberation to righteousness (a right standing before God) is envisioned as a form of Christ-centred enslavement (for example, Rom. 6.15–23). Jesus' return is imminent but believers are still encouraged to keep at work and not change the circumstances in which they were called (for example, 1 Cor. 7.21–24). Not only does Paul acknowledge the culture of enslavement that permeates the world in which he lives, but he also understands enslavement to be fundamental to a believer's loyalty to Christ. Enslavement, for Paul, is not simply a cultural system but a divinely ordained hierarchical system, fundamental to the God of Israel's rule and reign over the cosmos.

Reception: Paul, past and present

The figure of Paul and the Letters

Since the letters have been traditionally associated primarily with Paul, receptions of the letters are largely focused on him. Based on an analysis of the consistency between content, style, and theology, not all scholars think that every letter ascribed to Paul in the New Testament was written by the historical Paul. Rather, many scholars argue that some were written by those closely associated with him or simply by those who wanted to use his name to pass their ideas as authoritative (a process known as pseudepigraphy, explored in Chapters 5 and 7). Paul's letters are often divided into three main categories:

1. Undisputed: Romans, 1–2 Corinthians, Galatians, Philippians, 1 Thessalonians, Philemon;
2. Deutero-Pauline: Ephesians, Colossians, 2 Thessalonians;
3. The Pastoral Epistles: 1–2 Timothy, Titus.

Categories 2 and 3, including their scholarly reception, are treated in more detail in the next chapter and, as it will show, no scholarly consensus exists about the historical authenticity of the letters. Some scholars think that Colossians was written by Paul, others that both Ephesians and Colossians are authentic (again, more in the next chapter). Still others, that all 13 letters are from Paul's hand. Therefore, readers should be wary of any global claims about Pauline authorship and authenticity.

For those scholars convinced that only some of the letters with Paul's name in the New Testament were penned by the historical Paul, there is a 'Deutero-Pauline Paul' or a 'Paul of the Pastoral Epistles', and even a 'Paul of the Acts of the Apostles'. Scholars use this language to distinguish between the historical figure 'Paul' and the 'Pauls' who have been created by other unknown early Christian authors. The way interpreters understand the relationship between the letters of Paul and the historical person of Paul will affect the way those letters are interpreted. For example, depending on how one understands the authorship of the Pauline letters will also affect their dating. If all 13 letters originate with the historical Paul, then they were written between AD 40–60 (more precise dating depends on very complex arguments of chronology that cannot be rehearsed here). If one follows the threefold categorization of Paul's letters, then the undisputed letters are dated from the 40s to the 60s, the Deutero-Paulines to a post-60 context, and the Pastorals are from the later first- perhaps even second-century AD environment.

The many different Pauls of the New Testament are not the only Pauls that exist. Paul's letters, like much of the early Christian literature that later was canonized, generated a whole network of other literature connected to Paul's life, name, and authority. Christians were inspired to extend, continue, and alter authoritative texts. Earlier generations of Christians within the first millennium AD attributed Pauline authorship to other texts, such as the Letter to the Hebrews, as argued by the second-/ third-century Church father Origen of Alexandria (see Chapter 6), and a third letter to the Corinthians (e.g. the fourth-century Syriac church). In addition to 3 *Corinthians*, there is a correspondence between Paul and the first-century Stoic philosopher Lucius Annaeus Seneca 'the Younger'. There is also an extended Acts-like work called the *Acts of Paul and Thecla*, which narrates a story about a woman named Thecla as she follows Paul through various Mediterranean cities (Paul plays a relatively secondary role in the work). Curious about how Paul died, early Christians wrote a *Martyrdom of Paul* that details his arrest in Rome and later beheading at the hands of Emperor Nero.

Scholars generally view these extra-canonical texts (literature outside the New Testament canon) as being spurious – that is they do not think that they have any connection with actual historical events. Although literature such as the *Martyrdom of Paul* and the *Acts of Paul and Thecla* contain romanticizations and embellishments, and even fiction/myth, there is still the possibility that they may contain some historically plausible features. Ancient Christian historians such as Eusebius of Caesarea, for example, affirmed Paul's death under Nero by beheading (*Ecclesiastical History* 2.25).

Paul's letters are thought to be some of the earliest Christian writings in existence, although recent work on New Testament chronology might shift that perspective in the coming years (for example, Bernier, 2022). We do know that they were some of the first to be collected and used authoritatively by some other early Christians in the late first/early second century AD (for example, 2 Pet. 3.15–16; Ignatius of Antioch, Polycarp, and Marcion of Sinope). Many hypotheses have been given over the years about how the 'collection' of Paul's letters came about, whether through Paul himself or by benefactors or co-workers at a major assembly like Corinth or Ephesus. However, a lot of our evidence comes from the second and third century onward. For example, the idea that Paul's letters first circulated in a ten-letter collection is based largely on Marcion of Sinope's use of only ten letters (found in Tertullian, *Against Marcion* 5) as well as our earliest manuscript of Paul's letters: Papyrus 46 (dating to the second–third centuries AD). While these documents show some use of Paul's letters, they by no means confirm that a singular collection ever existed (for more, see Lieu, 2018, pp. 779–98). It was likely economical to group Paul's letters together, but we simply do not have evidence for a singular authoritative collection of Paul's letters in the first century. It is in the second century that the 13-letter collection now in modern New Testaments clearly emerges.

As Paul's letters were copied by hand and reproduced over hundreds of years until the printing press, they were not transmitted alone. In medieval manuscripts of Paul's letters (which are often accompanied by the Acts of the Apostles and the Catholic Epistles), they are introduced by *Euthaliana*, a set of introductory materials to help guide readers (e.g. Monastery of the Lavra, Athos, GA 1751). These extra materials (sometimes called para-textual features) include a prologue, an introduction to the content of the letter, citations, and even an account of Paul's travels and his martyrdom in Rome (for details, see Scherbenske, 2013).

Surprisingly, Paul is one of the few figures in the New Testament who we have a physical description of early in our sources. In the *Acts of Paul and Thecla*, Paul is described as 'a small man with regard to height, bald on the head, curved in the legs, healthy, monobrowed, to a little degree – an aquiline nose, full of grace' (*Acts of Paul and Thecla* 3). I have argued that the physical description of Paul in the *Acts of Paul and Thecla* is historically plausible (see Soon, 2021). Depictions of Paul exist from the fourth century AD onward in a variety of visual cultures across the Mediterranean world. He appears on catacomb roofs, in mosaics, on sarcophagi, and even on gilded glass bowls and spoons. Although his image is not homogenous, often he appears as a bald man with a pointed beard, the earliest extant example being a wall painting in the catacombs of Santa Tecla, Rome. Paul's unimpressive image may reflect his unappealing physique noted by the Corinthian assembly (see 2 Cor. 10.1, 10). Some portraits of Paul even appear in medieval manuscripts at the beginning of epistles (e.g. Monastery of the Lavra, Athos, GA 1751, fol. 64v; National Library of Greece, Athens, GA 1875, fols 103r and 143r). These images serve as navigational markers (like bookmarks) to help readers navigate large documents without having to read every title (for more see, Eleen, 1982; Soon, 2022).

Figure 4.1 Unknown artist, Apostle Paul, 1479, Manuscript illumination, Monastery of the Lavra (Mount Athas), K.190, fol. 64v (GA 1751). Public domain image made available by the Library of Congress Collection of Manuscripts from the Monasteries of Mt Athos.

New readings of Paul and the Letters

Recent scholarship on Paul has focused on the reception of Paul from communities and perspectives that either have in the past been ignored or insufficiently theorized in the interpretation of his letters. I will now sketch seven exciting new areas where Pauline scholars are innovating.

Pauline interpretation since the eighteenth century has been dominated by white interpreters from Europe and North America. Scholars, such as Lisa M. Bowens in her work *African American Readings of Paul* (2020), are working to recover the historical and theological use of Paul's letters by African American communities from the nineteenth to twentieth centuries in North America. Interpreters like Jupiter Hammon, Lemuel Haynes, Jarena Lee, Zilpha Elaw, Maria Stewart, Julia Foote, and Harriet Jacobs, among many others, are part of a neglected catalogue of Pauline interpreters whose insight and lived experience with his letters can reshape our understanding of these writings in both their historical context and contemporary use. The recovery of Pauline receptions not just from among African Americans but from among Asian, Indigenous and BIPOC (Black, Indigenous, and People of Colour) communities globally provides a welcome alternative to the useful but limited published work of scholars in periodicals and monographs over the past 300 years.

One long-lasting consequence of certain interpretations of Paul has been the mistreatment of Jewish people. From very early on in the Christian tradition, Paul's gospel was thought to be antithetical to ancient forms of Judaism. This antithesis between Paul and ancient Judaism(s) reached its apex in the nineteenth century in the work of Ferdinand Christian Baur. After the horrors of the Holocaust and the prolonged use of the New Testament to reinforce antisemitism among European and North American scholars, a new generation of twentieth-century scholars beginning with Krister Stendahl, E. P. Sanders, and James Dunn began to reread Jewish literature from the Second Temple period and the rabbis. This eventually led to new perspectives on Paul that began to read him as coherent within his ancient Jewish context. Recently, there has been a turn towards reading Paul fully within ancient Judaism (sometimes called the 'radical perspective on Paul' but more accurately termed 'Paul within Judaism'). Paula Fredriksen in *Paul: The Pagans' Apostle* (2017) writes at the forefront of this movement, arguing that Paul does not abandon the Jewish law or Judaism for 'Christianity' but that he operates fully within an apocalyptic worldview grounded in ancient Judaism itself. Far from portraying Paul as the founder of Christianity, Fredriksen portrays Paul as a Second Temple Jewish teacher grappling with the mass inclusion of non-Jews in a thoroughly Jewish movement driven by Jesus as Messiah.

While Fredriksen and others who work under the banner of Paul within Judaism analyse Paul primarily in his ancient Jewish context, some scholars, such as John Kloppenborg (2019), examine the social nature of Pauline communities in the wider ancient world (although not neglecting Jewish sources). Kloppenborg stands in the tradition of Wayne Meeks whose book *The First Urban Christians* (1983) was a watershed study into the social world of Paul the Apostle. In his focus on ancient associations as an analogy to early Christian communities, Kloppenborg turns towards the documentary and archaeological evidence available to sketch the way these assemblies functioned, the spaces in which they met, and how members expressed belonging with each other. This comparative work brings insight to Paul's rhetoric around meals and his monetary collection to Jerusalem.

Some of the most exciting new work on Paul is being done from the perspectives of gender and disability. Recently, Grace Emmett, in her dissertation 'Becoming a Man: Un/Manly Presentation in the Pauline Epistles' (2021), has examined Paul's self-presentation in his letters in conversation with ancient standards of masculinity. She explores the ways that Paul's use of bodily weakness, his physical scars, self-enslavement, and maternal metaphors teeter between manly *and* unmanly masculinities. Paul can, therefore, be read as a paradoxical man whose gender fluctuates constantly in relation to an interpreter's own conceptions of masculinity.

Scholarship is exploring how Paul's paradox of weakness and strength also affect his conception and use of disability and impairment. My own interests particularly lie in how Paul can be analysed in conversation with contemporary disability studies to uncover how he was disabled (Soon, 2023). As mentioned above, the description in the *Acts of Paul and Thecla* may have more historical credibility than previously thought, and when read through the lens of historical disability, it is plausible to understand Paul as someone who lived with dwarfism. Paul can be read as a disabled apostle in more ways than one, but what is more important than the specific diagnoses and conditions that he had is the way that he participates in the stigmatization of his own bodily conditions. Reading Paul with disability in mind opens new avenues to explore embodiment, mental health, and the diversity of lived experiences in the ancient world. More importantly, however, thinking about Paul through disability enables readers to reassess presuppositions they have towards the bodies of early Christian figures such as Paul, Jesus, and other apostles.

Finally, some of the recent scholarly focus on Paul has been how his texts should be used today apart from a necessarily religious use. New Testament scholars Cavan Concannon and Joseph Marchal offer two possible ways forward. For Marchal in *Appalling Bodies* (2019), what is interesting about Paul's letters is less so Paul himself and what he necessarily intended in his writing (an elusive goal that shifts with each passing generation), than the figures who are affected, stigmatized, and maligned by Paul's rhetoric. Marchal centres prophetic women, castrated men, the enslaved, and 'barbarians', analysing Paul's use and portrayal of them in their ancient social world and also exploring these uses and portrayals through contemporary queer and feminist perspectives (not just theory but also culture). Where Marchal focuses on bringing the contemporary world into the past, Concannon's *Profaning Paul* (2021) brings the reality of Paul's letters to the present, homing in on Paul's arguments that keep women in subjugation, slavery in place, and allow men to retain ancient levels of patriarchy. Concannon implicates New Testament scholars today for their selective readings of Paul that ignore the underlying frameworks incompatible with the modern world. Therefore, both Marchal and Concannon press new generations of readers to confront the many ways Paul's letters are used to harm people and reminds them that every interpretation of Paul is ethical and consequential.

Recommended further reading

Barnewall, Michelle, 2006, *Paul, the Stoics, and the Body of Christ*, SNTSMS 137; Cambridge: Cambridge University Press.

Bowens, Lisa M., 2020, *African American Readings of Paul: Reception, Resistance, and Transformation*, Grand Rapids, MI: Eerdmans.

Fredriksen, Paula, 2017, *Paul: The Pagans' Apostle*, New Haven, CT: Yale University Press.

Hodge, Caroline Johnson, 2007, *If Sons, Then Heirs: A Study of Kinship and Ethnicity in the Letters of Paul*, Oxford: Oxford University Press.

Strawbridge, Jennifer R., 2016, *The Pauline Effect: The Use of the Pauline Epistles by Early Christian Writers*, Studies of the Bible and its Reception 5; de Gruyter: Berlin.

Tupamahu, Ekaputra, 2023, *Contesting Languages: Heteroglossia and the Politics of Language in the Early Church*, New York: Oxford University Press.

References

Baur, Ferdinand Christian, 1867, *Paulus, der Apostel Jesu Christi; sein Leben und Wirken, seine Briefe und seine Lehre. Ein Beitrag zu einer kritischen Geschichte des Urchristenthums*, Leipzig: Fues's Verlag (L.W. Reisland).

Bernier, Jonathan, 2022, *Rethinking the Dates of the New Testament: The Evidence for Early Composition*, Grand Rapids, MI: Baker Academic.

Bowens, Lisa M., 2020, *African American Readings of Paul: Reception, Resistance, and Transformation*, Grand Rapids, MI: Eerdmans.

Concannon, Cavan W., 2021, *Profaning Paul*, Chicago, IL: University of Chicago Press.

Dunn, James D. G., 1983, 'The New Perspective on Paul', *Bulletin of the John Rylands Library*, 65, pp. 95–122.

Eleen, Luba, 1982, *The Illustration of the Pauline Epistles in French and English Bibles of the Twelfth and Thirteenth Centuries*, Oxford: Clarendon Press.

Emmett, Grace E., 2021, 'Becoming a Man: Un/Manly Self-Presentation in the Pauline Epistles', unpublished PhD diss., King's College London.

Fredriksen, Paula, 2017, *Paul: The Pagans' Apostle*, New Haven, CT: Yale University Press.

Kloppenborg, John S., 2019, *Christ's Associations: Connecting and Belonging in the Ancient City*, New Haven, CT: Yale University Press.

Lieu, Judith M., 2018, 'Marcion and the Canonical Paul', in Jens Schröter, et al. (eds), *Receptions of Paul in Early Christianity: The Person of Paul and His Writings Through the Eyes of His Early Interpreters*, Berlin: De Gruyter, pp. 779–98.

Marchal, Joseph A., 2019, *Appalling Bodies: Queer Figures Before and After Paul's Letters*, Oxford: Oxford University Press.

Meeks, Wayne A., 1983, *The First Urban Christians: The Social World of the Apostle Paul*, New Haven, CT: Yale University Press.

Moss, Candida R., 2023, 'The Secretary: Enslaved Workers, Stenography, and the Production of Early Christian Literature', *Journal of Theological Studies*, 74 1, pp. 20–56.

Sanders, E. P., 1977, *Paul and Palestinian Judaism: A Comparison of Patterns of Religion*, Minneapolis, MN: Fortress Press.

———, 1985, *Jesus and Judaism*, Philadelphia, PA: Fortress Press.

Scherbenske, Eric W., 2013, *Canonizing Paul: Ancient Editorial Practice and the Corpus Paulinum*, Oxford: Oxford University Press.

Soon, Isaac T., 2023, *A Disabled Apostle: Impairment and Disability in the Letters of Paul*, Oxford: Oxford University Press.

———, 2022, 'Absent in Body, Present in Spirit: Apostolic Iconography in Greek Byzantine New Testament Manuscripts', *Religions*, 13 7, p. 574.

———, 2021, 'The Short Apostle: The Stature of Paul in Light of 2 Cor 11:33 and the Acts of Paul and Thecla', *Early Christianity*, 12 2, pp. 159–78.

Stendahl, Krister, 1963, 'The Apostle Paul and the Introspective Conscience of the West', *Harvard Theological Review*, 56 3, pp. 199–215.

5

The 'Deutero-Pauline' Epistles

MICHAEL SCOTT ROBERTSON

This chapter focuses on a specific group of the Pauline Epistles known as the Deutero-Pauline Epistles, showcasing key scholarly theories concerning New Testament authorship. The Deutero-Pauline Epistles are a group of six documents that claim Pauline authorship, but modern biblical scholars have determined that, with varying degrees of confidence, Paul did not write them. The Deutero-Pauline Epistles consist of: 2 Thessalonians, Colossians, Ephesians, 1 and 2 Timothy, and Titus. The latter three constitute a further subdivision: the 'Pastoral Epistles'. As these letters and their connection to Pauline studies has already been outlined in the previous chapter, the ensuing discussion will not repeat that material here (see Chapter 4 for overviews).

This chapter is interested in the way that scholarly readers have engaged with this subgroup of Pauline Epistles. Therefore, after an overview of key themes, I focus on scholarly debates about authorship, first looking at 2 Thessalonians, Colossians, and Ephesians, and then the Pastoral Epistles. I also explain the important concept of pseudepigraphy which was widely practised in the ancient world (see also Chapter 7). In doing so, this chapter allows us to see the history of an idea: the idea that these letters were not written by Paul, and to trace the reception of this idea and its impact on current scholarly views.

Key themes

Cosmic events

For both Colossians and Ephesians, the interpretation of the Christ event is as a cosmic one. In Colossians, the first half of the letter contains two main sections that discuss Christ and his cosmic power over all creation. Scholars such as Harry O. Maier (2005) have demonstrated how this draws on Roman emperor worship as a paradigm for portrayals of Christ.

The author depicts Christ as one in whom deity dwells and who is a higher authority than all others. In Ephesians, the letter says that Christ was seated in the heavenly places (1.15–23). The cosmic nature of the Christ event is extended to the meaning of this event for those who believe in Christ. Those who believe are involved in a cosmic struggle with the prince of the power of the air (2.2), thus giving their lives cosmic implications. They, along with Christ, are seated in heaven (2.7), placing those who receive the letter in the cosmic sphere. Thus, in both these epistles, the gospel and those who believe in the gospel are given cosmic significance.

Church order

In 1 Timothy and Titus, the overarching theme is church order. The letters contain several sections on how people are to relate to the group, such as bishops, women, men, and widows (1 Timothy 3.1–12; 5; Titus 2.1–10). A key theme that has received considerable scholarly attention is the place of women within these early groups of Jesus' followers. 1 Timothy 2.8–15 delineates the author's ideal that women should not teach or have authority over men because of their connection to the first woman – Eve. Further, the author links women's childbearing to salvation (2.15). The issues in this passage are complicated by the irregular grammar, making it difficult to discern the subject of the verbs throughout 2.9–15. What is clear is that for 1 Timothy, the theme of church order finds its centre in the metaphor of the household (3.15). Thus, within 1 Timothy, the themes of household and church overlap and interpenetrate one another such that the church is the 'household of God' (Roitto, 2008). This relationship between church and household is also important in Ephesians, where the (authoritative) relationship between the husband and wife is drawn as a parallel between Christ and the church (5.21—6.9). In this parallel, however, the author claims to use the husband/wife relationship as an illustration to illuminate his concept of the relationship between Christ and the church. Colossians, in a similar way to Ephesians, presents the Greco-Roman ideal for the household (submission to a male authority) following the literary tradition of household codes stretching back to at least Aristotle (*Politics*, 1.2.1–2), slightly adapted to life for the believer (3.18—4.1; for more see MacDonald, 2007; Kartzow, 2010).

End times and passing on

In both 2 Timothy and 2 Thessalonians, there is a strong emphasis on the end times. For the author of 2 Thessalonians, there will be a rebellion and a lawless one that will precede Jesus. They claim that the spirit of lawlessness is currently at work in the world, but someone is holding it back from its full and final manifestation of wickedness (2.7). The author of 2 Timothy sees the end times as one of great debauchery within the group (3.1–9; 4.1–8).

The author of 2 Timothy is concerned about a different end: the end of their own life (4.6), as the letter focuses on fulfilling and passing on the Pauline ministry. Indeed, information about the 'person of Paul' is intertwined into all these letters. As well as claiming to be passing on his last wishes in 2 Timothy, Paul claims to sign in his own hand (2 Thess. 3.17; Col. 4.18). Also, Paul's receiving of unique revelations is enhanced in Ephesians. The author calls these revelations 'mysteries', parts of the divine plan that were concealed before Christ but made known to Paul. In this letter, it is only through Paul that these mysteries come to light. Colossians 1.2–27 echoes these sentiments. Direct connection to Paul is so important for these authors that 2 Thessalonians even acknowledges pseudepigraphy within the early Jesus movement: in 2.2 the author mentions the possibility of a letter circulating which claims to be from Paul, Timothy, and Silvanus that contains teaching contrary to that of the author.

Reception: Who really wrote these Letters?

2 Thessalonians, Colossians, and Ephesians

In antiquity, the three Deutero-Pauline letters – 2 Thessalonians, Colossians, and Ephesians – were considered to be written by Paul himself. Marcion (d.c. AD 160) included all three in his canon, and they are listed among the accepted books in the late second-century Muratorian Canon.

Ephesians and Colossians were the first of the three to have their authenticity questioned. In the late 1700s, English clergyman Edward Evanson (who also questioned the authenticity of the Pastoral Epistles) denied that Paul wrote them because of the dissonance between these letters and Acts. In his *The Dissonance of the Four Generally Received Evangelists, and the Evidence of their Respective Authenticity Examined* (1792), Evanson said that based on Acts 18 and 19, Paul preached the gospel in Ephesus.

However, Ephesians 1.15–16 indicates that Paul had only heard of the faith of the Ephesians rather than experienced it himself. Evanson made essentially the same argument against Colossians. Colossians 1.4–9 says that Epaphras, rather than Paul, was the one to first preach the gospel to them, but Acts 16.6—18.23 says that Paul did visit Phrygia, the region in which Colossae was situated.

In 1838, Ernst Meyerhoff advanced a series of arguments against the authenticity of Colossians by noting that the style, language, and vocabulary differed from Paul's undisputed writings. Meyerhoff claimed that the opponents in the letter postdated the time of Paul considerably. He also doubted the authenticity of Colossians based upon the close similarity between it and Ephesians.

The authorship of 2 Thessalonians was first questioned by Johann Ernst Christian Schmidt in 1801. Schmidt argued that the divergence in eschatology between 1 and 2 Thessalonians was too great for both to have been written by Paul and that the warning against forgeries in 2.1–12 was unpauline. This criticism was followed in 1829 by Friedrich Heinrich Kern, who argued that 2 Thessalonians was dependent upon 1 Thessalonians, and that 3.17 was particularly unpauline.

Ferdinand Christian Baur's work in the mid-nineteenth century maintains a particularly important position within the reception of the Deutero-Paulines. Agreeing with many of the arguments above (and extending them to Ephesians), Baur systematized their pseudonymity by creating a reconstruction of early Christianity that places each letter within the developing movement. Baur only accepted four letters as authentically Pauline – Romans, 1 and 2 Corinthians, and Galatians. He doubted 2 Thessalonians, based on his idea that the apocalypticism of chapter 2 was more like Jewish Christianity than Paulinism. He also saw 2 Thessalonians as too different from 2 Corinthians 15 for Paul to have written both (for more, see Thiselton, 2011). In addition, Bauer placed Colossians and Ephesians in the second century as writings against Gnosticism. As a result of these examinations, although scholars would come to accept Philippians, Philemon, and 1 Thessalonians as authentic, 2 Thessalonians, Colossians, and Ephesians would remain in doubt and be considered part of the Deutero-Paulines.

Today, the authorship of these three letters is still contested. Unlike the Pastoral Epistles, 2 Thessalonians, Colossians, and Ephesians have many scholars arguing for their authenticity. However, many continue to see these as Deutero-Pauline and most scholars conceive of the Deutero-Paulines as part of a developing Pauline School (for more, see MacDonald 2014).

Pseudepigraphy

How could these writings claim to be by Paul and include such intimate details about him, and yet not be written by him? We have seen that the author of 2 Thessalonians raises the issue of pseudepigraphy in their work. Pseudepigraphy is the act of falsely attributing authorship to a written work. Similarly, a work written under a false name is called a pseudepigraphon. (A closely related phenomenon is pseudonymity, which is writing under a false name.)

That pseudepigraphy was ubiquitous in the Greco-Roman world is demonstrated by numerous writers who recorded that it was taking place. For example, the second-century physician Galen said of the fifth- to fourth-century BC physician Hippocrates' work *On the Nature of Man*:

> [B]efore the kings of Alexandria and Pergamon became so ambitious to possess ancient books, authorship was never falsely attributed. However, after the ones who collected the writings of a given ancient author for these kings first received a reward for this, they immediately collected many works, which they falsely inscribed.

Although Galen's account of when pseudepigraphy began is likely erroneous, the passage shows that people in the Greco-Roman world were keenly aware that pseudepigraphy was a common phenomenon. They were so aware of it that Galen felt the need to include this digression in his writing.

Pseudepigraphy was also widespread among Jewish documents. A particularly famous example are the works that comprise *1 Enoch*. In the beginning of *1 Enoch*, the document claims to have been written by Enoch, the seventh in the line of Adam. This Enoch lived, according to Genesis 5.18–24, before the great flood. The earliest layer of *1 Enoch*, however, was not written until the third century BC, placing it well beyond the lifetime of its purported author. Many other Jewish pseudepigrapha are known, such as: *Testaments of the Twelve Patriarchs*, *Odes of Solomon*, *4 Ezra*, and *The Apocalypse of Abraham*.

The widespread nature of pseudepigraphy raises the question, why would authors have written under false names? The quote from Galen above shows that one reason was for financial gain. Authors would sell works that they had written by falsely ascribing them to another, more famous author. The third- to fourth-century philosopher Iamblichus said that some philosophers wrote under the name of more famous philosophers, and unlike Galen, he had a favourable opinion of this practice (*Life of Pythagoras*, 31.198). The second- to third-century church father Tertullian claimed that the author of the *Acts of Paul and Thecla* said he wrote this work because he loved Paul (*On Baptism*, 17). Tertullian, however, disapproved. Thus, there were several reasons for writing under a false name, and there were likely many more than listed here. What is more, the above instances show that there was a range of opinions as to the acceptability of writing pseudepigrapha. Galen and Tertullian gave negative evaluations of the instances they wrote about, while Iamblichus and the author of the *Acts of Paul and Thecla* seem to have had positive views of at least some instances of pseudepigraphy. The overwhelming majority, however, did not approve.

One aspect of the reception of pseudepigrapha requires specific attention. The Epistle of Jude in the New Testament cites the pseudepigraphon *1 Enoch* as authoritative scripture (for more, see Chapter 7). Jude 14–15 says:

> It was also about these that Enoch, in the seventh generation from Adam, prophesied, saying, 'See, the Lord is coming with ten thousands of his holy ones, to execute judgment on all, and to convict everyone of all the deeds of ungodliness that they have committed in such an ungodly way, and of all the harsh things that ungodly sinners have spoken against him.

The citation is from *1 Enoch* 1.9, and Jude quotes it as if it were the actual Enoch himself speaking. Whether the author of Jude knew that *1 Enoch* was a pseudepigraphon or not is unknown, but it does show that the authors of the New Testament did accept some pseudepigrapha as carrying authority.

Pseudepigraphy was practised in early Christianity. Documents such as *3 Corinthians*, which claims to be written by Paul, were well known not to have been written by the Apostle. Other examples include the *Letter of Pseudo-Titus* and the letters of Paul to Seneca and, as already noted, 2 Thessalonians acknowledges that there were likely pseudepigraphic letters circulating in Paul's name.

Today, most scholars agree that there are pseudepigrapha in the New Testament. Even though the authorship of 2 Thessalonians, Colossians, and Ephesians is highly debated within scholarship, many scholars consider one or more of these three to be authentic Pauline writings. However, we shall now see that scholars are more settled in their determination of the inauthenticity of 1 and 2 Timothy, and Titus: the Pastoral Epistles.

The Pastoral Epistles

Designating 1 Timothy, 2 Timothy, and Titus as 'Pastoral Epistles' was instigated in the thirteenth century by Thomas Aquinas' comment that 1 Timothy was 'virtually a pastoral rule' (*In omnes S. Pauli Apostoli epistolas commentaria*, 1 Tim. 1.4). In 1703, D. N. Berdot called Titus a Pastoral Epistle, and, in 1753, Paul Anton noted that these three letters were commonly called the Pastoral Epistles.

In antiquity, the Pastoral Epistles were mostly, but not exclusively, received as authentic Pauline writings. Origen (d.c. AD 254) noted that some did not consider 2 Timothy authentic (*Commentaria in Evangelium secundum Matthaeum* PL 13.176). Clement of Alexandria (d.c. AD 215) said that some heretics rejected the letters to Timothy (*Stromata*, 2.11.52). Augustine (d. AD 430) claimed that Faustus did not hold to Pauline authorship of Titus (*Contra Faustum*, 21.1). In the fourth and second century respectively, Jerome (*Commentary on Titus*, Preface) and Tertullian (*Against Marcion*, 5.21) said that Marcion did not think that Paul wrote 1 and 2 Timothy or Titus. Most, however, did not question these documents' claim to Pauline authorship.

Since the early doubters in antiquity, the Pauline authorship of the Pastorals was not questioned again until 1792, when Evanson raised the possibility that Paul did not write Titus. He based his assessment on four issues: 1. the language of the introduction is different from the other Pauline letters; 2. the slander in Titus 1.12 is unpauline in character; 3. the state of the church in Titus fits better after the time of Paul; and 4. Titus 3.3 includes Paul among those who led morally reprehensible lives unlike the other Paulines.

After Evanson, in 1808 Friedrich Schleiermacher argued that 1 Timothy was not written by Paul. His argument was based upon the lack of references to 1 Timothy in the early Apostolic Fathers and the distinct language of the letter compared to the other Pauline letters. In 1812, Johann Gottfried Eichhorn called into question all three of the Pastoral Epistles by expanding Schleiermacher's method to 2 Timothy and Titus. In 1845, Baur placed them after the lifetime of Paul by connecting the polemic in the letters to arguments against Marcion. Heinrich Holtzmann, writing in 1880, accepted that the Pastorals were not written by Paul, but he tied the three together into what he calls 'inseparable triples'. This had the effect of not only advancing the idea that Paul did not write the Pastorals, but it also brought these three documents together as a distinct corpus. P. N. Harrison, in *The Problem of the Pastoral Epistles* (1921), expanded the linguistic argument against the authenticity of the Pastorals. By this point, the majority of scholars were convinced that the Pastoral Epistles were a corpus that was not written by Paul himself, and this remains true today (for more, see Johnson, 1996).

Today, scholars view the Pastoral Epistles as a late, culturally conservative, example of the Pauline School. For much of the nineteenth to twenty-first centuries, they have been viewed as examples of 'Early Catholicism', where the apocalyptic hope of earlier Paulinism has faded, and the author of the Pastorals is forced to contend with a long stay in the world before the return of Jesus (for example, Käsemann, 1969). Martin Dibelius and Hans Conzelmann have argued that this resulted in 'bourgeois Christianity', where the author of the Pastorals co-opted the ethics of the surrounding culture. However, scholars such as T. Christopher Hoklotubbe (2017) and Dogara Ishaya Manomi (2021) now tend to see this as more nuanced, showing that while the author adapted the Pauline message to a new situation and incorporated Greco-Roman ethics, they nevertheless adapted these ethics to the message of the gospel.

Questions today: Date, author, provenance

The questions of date, author, and location for each New Testament document is a central part of scholarly understanding. How, then, do the above debates impact how these letters are understood today? Due to the more widespread consensus of pseudonymity, we shall focus on the Pastoral Epistles to demonstrate the factors used to try and ascertain this information.

The date of the composition of the Pastoral Epistles is difficult to discover with certainty. Although the small minority of scholars who view the Pastorals as authentically Pauline will date them to the late AD 50s–60s (see Kelly, 1960; Moo and Carson, 2005), many tend to date them into the second century. There are a number of reasons for this conclusion. The first is that the language used in the Pastoral Epistles is quite different from that of the undisputed Pauline letters. Many words are used in the Pastorals that Paul never uses, and these unique words in the Pastoral Epistles, such as ἁγνεία (hagneia), γάγγραινα (gangraina), and νομικός (nomikos), are more characteristic of the late first to second century than that of Paul's time (for more, see Collins, 2002; Harrison, 1921). Further, the organization of the group has developed beyond Paul's limited organizational scheme. The discussions of bishops, elders, and priests in the Pastoral Epistles fit more closely with the Apostolic Fathers of the late first to early second century such as *1 Clement*, Polycarp, and Ignatius (see MacDonald, 1988).

Another argument for the late date of the Pastorals comes from their reception in the early church. Marcion, writing in the early second century, famously did not have the Pastorals in his Pauline canon. Although some church fathers, such as Tertullian (*Against Marcion*, 5.21.1) and Jerome (*Commentary on Titus*, Prologue), claimed that Marcion intentionally omitted these letters, it is more likely that they had not yet been written, and that Marcion, therefore, did not know them (Theobald, 2016; Von Harnack, 1924). One of the most persuasive points in favour of this interpretation is that, given Marcion's well-known anti-Jewish stance, it is unlikely that he would have omitted the Pastorals because of the rhetoric against 'those of the circumcision' in Titus 1.10 (Campbell, 2014, p. 390). Thus, when these arguments are weighed together, the evidence points towards a date for the writing of the Pastoral Epistles as somewhere in the early to mid-second century.

Most scholars consider the Pastoral Epistles to be pseudepigraphal – that is, although they claim Pauline authorship, they were written by someone else (for a defence of Pauline authorship, see Prior, 1989). A few scholars have proposed alternate authors, such as Luke, Timothy, or Polycarp (see Wilson, 1979; Bauckham, 1988), but most scholars allow the identity of the author to remain unknown. More debated, however, is the number of authors who contributed to the Pastoral Epistles. The majority opinion is that the three Pastorals were all written by a single author, but recently Jenz Herzer (2017) has advocated for a different author for 1 Timothy, and others such as W. A. Richards (2002) and P. Hofrichter (1987) suggest three or four contributors. Thus, although most consider the Pastorals to have a single author, this conclusion is currently under scrutiny, and it is not clear on which conclusion scholarship will coalesce in the future.

The Pastoral Epistles do not give much indication of their place of origin, but many scholars place their writing somewhere in the Roman province of Asia (for more see Zamfir, 2013, p. 8; Hoklotubbe, 2017, p. 14). Although the ostensible destination for 1 Timothy is Ephesus and Titus is Crete, the late date of the Pastorals means that these are likely not the actual destinations. This situation is known as double pseudonymity.

The Deutero-Paulines occupy a unique place within the canon. Although they claim that Paul wrote them, it is highly likely that they were written by someone else. As we have seen, this phenomenon of writing under a false name – pseudepigraphy – was common in the Greco-Roman world, and so it is no surprise that some pseudonymous writings became part of the New Testament. The Deutero-Paulines constitute a diverse set of letters and through engaging with their scholarly history, we can see the questions that readers have asked of them and the issues about the early church that they raise. We can also see how these debates help us to consider when, by whom, and where they may have been composed. However, regardless of the debates that surround them, these letters do have unifying features. They have, as Margaret MacDonald (2014) has pointed out, two unifying themes: they emphasize Paul's co-workers, and they focus on tradition. Both these factors mean that their import is still huge for those who read these letters within faith communities today.

Recommended further reading

Harrison, James R. and L. L. Welborn (eds), 2019, *The First Urban Churches 5: Colossae, Hierapolis, and Laodicea*, Atlanta, GA: SBL Press.

Hoklotubbe, T. Christopher, 2017, *Civilized Piety: The Rhetoric of Pietas in the Pastoral Epistles and the Roman Empire*, Waco, TX: Baylor University Press.

Maier, Harry O., 2013, *Picturing Paul in Empire: Imperial Image, Text and Persuasion in Colossians, Ephesians, and the Pastoral Epistles*, London: Bloomsbury.

Mitchell, Margaret M., 2017, *Paul and the Emergence of Christian Textuality: Early Christian Literary Culture in Context*, Tübingen: Mohr Siebeck.

Zamfir, Korinna, 2013, *Men and Women in the Household of God: A Contextual Approach to Roles and Ministries in the Pastoral Epistles*, Göttingen: Vandenhoeck & Ruprecht.

References

Anton, Paul, 1753, *Exegetische Abhandlung der Pastoral-Briefe Pauli an Timotheum und Titum im Jahr 1726 und 1727 Öffentlich Vorgetragen*, Halle: Wänsenhauses.

Bauckham, Richard, 1988, 'Pseudo-Apostolic Letters', *Journal of Biblical Literature*, 107 3, pp. 469–94.

Baur, Ferdinand Christian, 1845, *Paulus, der Apostel Jesu Christi; sein Leben und Wirken, seine Briefe und seine Lehre. Ein Beitrag zu einer kritischen Geschichte des Urchristenthums*, Stuttgart: Becher & Mülle.

———, 1876, *Paul, the Apostle of Jesus Christ, His Life and Work, His Epistles and His Doctrine*, London: Williams and Norgate, 1876.

Berdot, D. N., 1703, *Exercitatio Theologica Exegetica in Epistolam S. Pauli ad Titum*, Halle: Litteris Orphanotrophii.

Campbell, Douglas A., 2014, *Framing Paul: An Epistolary Biography*, Grand Rapids, MI: William B. Eerdmans.

Collins, Raymond F., 2002, *1 & 2 Timothy and Titus: A Commentary*, New Testament Library, Louisville, KY: Westminster John Knox.

Dibelius, Martin and Hans Conzelmann, 1972, *The Pastoral Epistles: A Commentary on the Pastoral Epistles*, Hermeneia, Philadelphia, PA: Fortress Press.

Eichhorn, J. G., 1812, *Einleitung in das Neue Testament*, vol. 1, Leipzig: Weidmannischen Buchhandlung, 3, pp. 315–410.

Evanson, Edward, 1792, *The Dissonance of the Four Generally Received Evangelists, and the Evidence of Their Respective Authenticity Examined*, Ipswich: Jermyn.

Harnack, Adolf von, 1924, *Marcion: Das Evangelium vom fremden Gott: Eine Monographie zur Geschichte der Grundlegung der katholischen Kirke*, Leipzig: J. C. Hinrichs.

Harrison, P. N., 1921, *The Problem of the Pastoral Epistles*, Oxford: Oxford University Press.

Herzer, Jens, 2017, 'Zwischen Mythos und Wahrheit: Neue Perspektiven auf die sogenannten Pastoralbriefe', *New Testament Studies*, 63 3, pp. 428–50.

Hofrichter, Peter L., 1987, 'Strukturdebatte im Namen des Apostels: Zur Abhängigkeit der Pastoralbriefe untereinander und vom ersten Petrusbrief', in N. Brox (ed.), *Anfänge der Theologie: ΧΑΡΙΣΤΕΙΟΝ Johannes B. Bauer Zum Jänner 1987*, Graz: Styria, pp. 101–16.

Hoklotubbe, T. Chrisopher, 2017, *Civilized Piety: The Rhetoric of Pietas in the Pastoral Epistles and the Roman Empire*, Waco, TX: Baylor University Press.

Holtzmann, H. J., 1880, *Die Pastoralbriefe, kritisch und exegetisch behandelt*, Leipzig: Engelmann.

Johnson, Luke Timothy, 1996, *Letters to Paul's Delegates: 1 Timothy, 2 Timothy, Titus*, Valley Forge: Trinity Press.

Kartzow, Marianne, 2010, '"Asking The Other Question": An Intersectional Approach To Galatians 3:28 And The Colossian Household Codes', *Biblical Interpretation*, 18 4–5, pp. 364–89.

Käsemann, Ernst, 1969, *New Testament Questions of Today*, trans. W. J. Montague, Philadelphia, PA: Fortress Press.

Kelly, J. N. D., 1960, *The Pastoral Epistles*, Black's New Testament Commentaries, Peabody, MA: Hendrickson.

Kern, F. H., 1839, 'Über II Thess. 2:1–12. Nebst Andeutungen über den Ursprung des zweiten Briefs an die Thessalonicher', *Tübinger Zeitschrift für Theologie*, 2, pp. 145–214.

Lewis, W. J., n.d., 'Galen, On Hippocrates's "On the Nature of Man"', https://www.ucl.ac.uk/~ucgajpd/medicina%20antiqua/tr_GnatHom.html, accessed 8.02.2022.

MacDonald, Margaret Y., 1988, *The Pauline Churches: A Socio-Historical Study of Institutionalization in the Pauline and Deutero-Pauline Writings*, Cambridge: Cambridge University Press.

——, 2007, 'Slavery, Sexuality and House Churches: A Reassessment of Colossians 3.18–4.1 in Light of New Research on the Roman Family', *New Testament Studies*, 53 1, pp. 94–113.

——, 2014, 'The Deutero-Pauline Letters in Contemporary Research', in Matthew V. Novenson and R. Barry Matlock (eds), *The Oxford Handbook of Pauline Studies*, Oxford: Oxford University Press.

Maier, Harry O., 2005, 'A Sly Civility: Colossians and Empire', *Journal for the Study of the New Testament*, 27 3, pp. 323–49.

Manomi, Dogara Ishaya, 2021, *Virtue Ethics in the Letter to Titus: An Inter-Disciplinary Study*, Tübingen: Mohr Siebeck.

Meyerhoff, Ernst, 1838, *Der Brief an die Colosser mit vornehmlicher Berücksichtigung der drei Pastoralbriefe*, Berlin: H. Schultze.

Moo, Douglas J. and D. A. Carson, 2005, *An Introduction to the New Testament*, 2nd edn, Grand Rapids, MI: Zondervan.

Prior, Michael, 1989, *Paul the Letter-Writer and the Second Letter to Timothy*, Sheffield: Continuum.

Richards, William A., 2002, *Difference and Distance in Post-Pauline Christianity: An Epistolary Analysis of the Pastorals*, New York: P. Lang.

Roitto, Rikard, 2008, 'Act as a Christ-Believer, as a Household Member or Both?: A Cognitive Perspective on the Relation Between the Social Identity in Christ and Household Identities in Pauline and Deutero-Pauline Texts', in Bengt Holmberg and Mikael Winninge (eds), *Identity Formation in the New Testament*, Tübingen: Mohr Siebeck, pp. 141–64.

Schleiermacher, F., 1807, *Über den sogennanten Ersten Brief des Paulus an den Timotheus: Ein kritisches Sendschreiben an Joachim Christian Gass*, Berlin: In der Realschulbuchhandlung.

Schmidt, Johann Ernst Christian, 1801, 'Vermuthungen über den beyden Briefe an die Thessalonicher', in Johann Ernst Christian Schmidt and Karl Christian Ludwig Schmidt (eds), *Bibliothek für Kritik und Exegese des Neuen Testaments und ältesten Christengeschichte*, Hadamar: Neue Gelehrtenbuchhandlung, 3.2, pp. 380–6.

Theobald, Michael, 2016, *Israel-Vergessenheit in den Pastoralbriefen: Ein neuer Vorschlag zu ihrer historisch-theologischen Verortung im 2. Jahrhundert n. Chr. unter besonderer Berücksichtigung der Ignatius-Briefe*, Stuttgart: Katholisches Bibelwerk.

Thiselton, Anthony C., 2011, *1 & 2 Thessalonians: Through the Centuries*, Chichester: Wiley-Blackwell.

Wilson, Stephen G., 1979, *Luke and the Pastoral Epistles*, London: SPCK.

Zamfir, Korinna, 2013, *Men and Women in the Household of God: A Contextual Approach to Roles and Ministries in the Pastoral Epistles*, Göttingen: Vandenhoeck & Ruprecht.

6

Hebrews

MICHELLE FLETCHER AND WEI HSIEN WAN

To speak of the 'non-Pauline' Epistles is, paradoxically, to underscore the importance of Paul not only in the New Testament canon, but also in the development of early Christianity as a whole. For much of Christian history, the 'non-Pauline' letters have taken a back seat in scholarship and preaching – a trend which, some would argue, continues today. While the non-Pauline texts have certainly not been as influential as the letters ascribed to Paul, this chapter (and the next on the Catholic Epistles) will show how they have, each in their own ways, played a key role in shaping Christian thought and practice. In this chapter, we focus on the text which begins 'To the Hebrews', which has a complicated relationship with the person of Paul. Despite this, we shall see how it has proven central in key theological battles, been used in vitriolic attacks on enemies, and been part of the long, complicated history of Jewish–Christian relations, with the book's emphasis on the 'superlative' covenant shaping Jewish–Christian relations in definitive, and too often destructive, ways. Finally, we shall showcase some of the ways it has become part of church life through feasts and artworks, as its themes continue to speak to lived experience.

Overview

Hebrews emphasizes God's revelation through his Son. It is through him that God has spoken in 'the last days' (1.2) and the Son has a place of cosmic significance, because it is through him that the cosmos was created (1.2). Hebrews proceeds to expound the Son's superiority over all earlier ministers of the covenant (1—4) and even the institution of the Israelite priesthood and its attendant economy of sacrificial worship (4.14—10.18). It creatively uses a wide variety of Hebrew Bible passages to do this.

Hebrews makes clear that Jesus surpasses the angels (1.5—2.17) owing to his sonship (1.5), the worship due to him (1.6–7), and his eternal enthronement (1.8–13). That this superior Jesus was fully human is made abundantly clear (2.5–18), as the author explains the need for Jesus to share the likeness of Abraham's descendants in order to be the pioneer of their salvation (2.10). With this paradox of superiority and humanness established, the importance of Jesus' death is foregrounded: it frees the addressees from the fear of death and renders Jesus as even more worthy than Moses (3.1–19) and Joshua (4.1–13). This is because he atones for the recipients' sins through his sacrifice and, as a result, is their eternal High Priest – subjects which are introduced in Hebrews 4 and 5 and expanded at length in Hebrews 7—10.18. To persuade the audience, the author employs complex allusions to the Jewish cultic system (8—10) and draws upon Genesis 14's presentation of the figure of Melchizedek and his invocation in Psalm 110 (Heb. 7; Gen. 14.18–20; Ps. 110.4).

Hebrews also makes clear the perils of unbelief, disobedience, and falling away which face the audience, providing warnings and exhortations (see 4.12–13; 5.11–14; 6.4–8) as well as reassurance and encouragement (see 4.16; 6.9–11,19–20). Indeed, the closing chapters of the book offer a sustained exhortation to persevere in faith (10.19—13.19), drawing from the examples of holy men and women in the scriptures of Israel (11.1–39), as well as of Jesus himself (12.1–13). With such examples to follow, the book closes with directions of how to live in a way that focuses on the city that is to come, sure in the eternal covenant.

Key themes

Superiority and remaining faithful

Hebrews quite decisively emphasizes two themes: 1. the uniqueness and superiority of God's revelation in Jesus over earlier forms and modes of revelation, and 2. the need to remain faithful in the path of discipleship.

The covenant established in Jesus is superior to the Mosaic in terms not only of its agents, both suprahuman (angels) and human (Moses, Joshua), but also in terms of its priesthood, tabernacle, and sacrifices. In fact, the text repeatedly expresses a fundamental conviction of the author: that the persons and rites of the Mosaic covenant were anticipatory forms (types) or 'copies' of the greater, heavenly things of Jesus' person and ministry (see 7.23–25; 9.23–28; 10.1). Tellingly, the Greek *kreittón*, usually translated as 'better', is used as a descriptor of Jesus' person and ministry 12 times in Hebrews. For the author, the surpassing nature of Jesus' covenant precisely deserves the readers' utmost loyalty.

This concern is first manifested in the author's habit of punctuating expository instruction with exhortations to faithfulness, usually marked off with a 'therefore' (for example at 2.1; 3.1; 4.1; 6.1). Then, in the longer call to faithfulness which makes up the second portion of the letter (10.19—13.19), the author argues from the lesser to the greater: if men and women of old such as Abraham, Sarah, Gideon, and David fought so hard to remain faithful to what was only promised but not given (11.39), how much more should his readers, now given those things in Jesus, push through every hardship and trial (12.12–24).

The coexistence of these two themes – the superiority of the new covenant and the need to persevere – have informed speculations regarding the situation facing the letter's original recipients. Although their precise circumstances remain unknown to us, many scholars believe it is probable that, in the author's view, his readers were on the verge of what amounted to an apostasy.

Reception: Readings of Hebrews

A Pauline text?

The letter in our manuscripts bears a set of apparently contradictory features. On the one hand, the absence of a prescript found in the other New Testament letters (that is, identifications of the author and recipients, along with some form of greeting and/or introduction), has led many scholars to regard Hebrews more as a sermon or homily than a letter as such. On the other hand, Hebrews 12.22–24 seems to be a letter postscript, complete with reference to a certain 'Timothy', perhaps even the well-known companion and protege of Paul. For many interpreters, both ancient and modern, this postscript is one of the key indicators of Pauline authorship – thus justifying the book's inclusion among the letters of Paul. Nevertheless, reflecting a greater scholarly consensus today, we include it among the non-Pauline texts (although it should be noted that this consensus is by no means always clear).

However, Hebrews also sits apart from the other 'non-Pauline Epistles' known as the Catholic Epistles (see Chapter 7) due to the very fact that it has a history of Pauline attribution. There was a consensus among Christian communities in the Eastern parts of the Roman Empire that it had in fact come from Paul. Among the Western churches, however, reservations about its authorship lingered until about the fourth century. After this, its Pauline attribution became more or less unchallenged.

Fig 6.1 Joannes Koulix (scribe), Leaf from the Epistle to the Hebrews, 1101, Tempera, gold and ink on parchment, 203 x 160 mm, The Metropolitan Museum of Art, New York, The Cloisters Collection, Rogers and Harris Brisbane Dick Funds, and Joseph Pulitzer Bequest, 1991, Accession Number: 1991.232.15, courtesy of www.metmuseum.org.

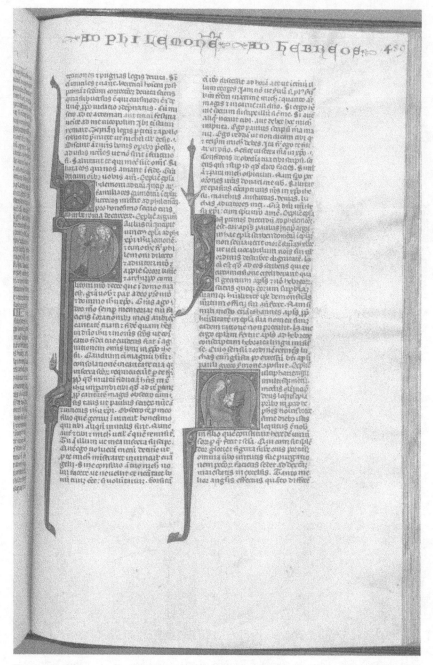

Fig 6.2 Unknown artist, Hebrews, historiated initial M, Paul seated at a desk, writing, c.1275–1300. Southern France, Toulouse(?). Ink, tempera, and gold on vellum,35.6 x 24.2 cm, The Cleveland Museum of Art, John L. Severance Fund, 2008.2.459, fol. 459r, courtesy of The Cleveland Museum of Art.

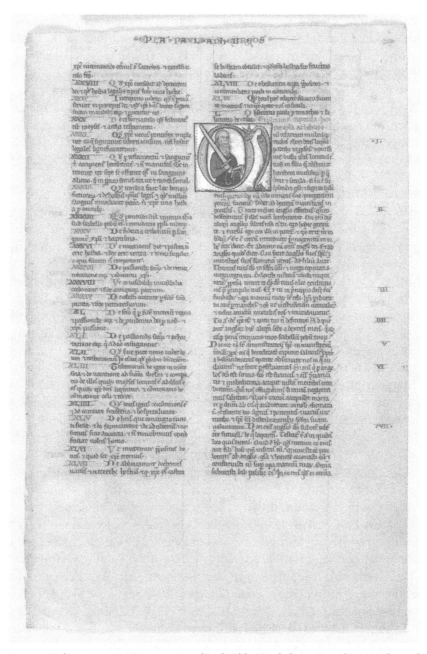

Fig 6.3 Unknown artist, Vienna Moralized Bible Workshop (French), Initial M of St Paul with a Sword and a Book, from a Latin Bible, c.1220. Ink, tempera, and burnished gold on vellum; 21.9 x 14.3 cm, The Cleveland Museum of Art, The Jeanne Miles Blackburn Collection, 2011.51, courtesy of The Cleveland Museum of Art.

As a result, we find Paul's image appearing at the start of Hebrews in both Greek and Latin manuscripts. For example, Joannes Koulix's twelfth-century, Byzantine-style Greek Praxapostolos (a New Testament minus the Gospels and Revelation) shows a small, illuminated bust of Paul to the left of Hebrews' opening verse (Metropolitan Museum of Art, New York; inv.no. 1991.232.15). In a thirteenth-century Latin manuscript from Southern France (Cleveland Museum of Art, inv.no. 2008.2, fol. 459r), the historiated (decorated) initial letter of Hebrews shows Paul seated at a writing desk, knife and quill in hand, composing the letter himself. Another folio from a thirteenth-century Bible from France (also Cleveland Museum of Art; inv. no. 2011.51) has the initial M (*Multifariam*) filled with Paul holding a sword, a paradigmatic representation of the Apostle. The sword identifies Paul because it is the symbol of his martyrdom, but here it also appropriately signals to the text's contents, as Hebrews 4.12 declares: 'Indeed, the word of God is living and active and sharper than any two-edged sword, piercing until it divides soul from spirit, joints from marrow'. Finally, another Latin Bible made in France in the second half of the thirteenth century (Morgan Library; MS M.970 fol. 409r) has the historiated initial M showing Paul teaching three men, each of whom wears a pointed hat, indicating to readers that Paul was preaching to the Jews.

Manuscript evidence is enlightening regarding the status of Hebrews as a Pauline epistle. Manuscripts show that it was included as part of the Pauline corpus, but that the position of Hebrews among Paul's letters evinces a high level of fluidity. For example, in the second-/third-century Papyrus 46 ($\mathfrak{P}$46), Hebrews appears between Romans and 1 Corinthians. In a ninth-century Sahidic manuscript (Morgan M570), it is placed after 2 Corinthians. In the fourth-century Codex Sinaiticus ($\aleph$) and fifth-century Codex Alexandrinus (A), it appears between 2 Thessalonians and 1 Timothy. However, it is the sixth-century Codex Claromontanus (D^p) which represents the tradition that would eventually predominate, with Hebrews appearing after Philemon, as the last of the Pauline Epistles.

This authorship consensus was, for the most part, undisturbed until the fifteenth century, when scholars began challenging the ascription to Paul based on the thematic and stylistic features of the letter. Although his authorship is debated, Paul may still have exercised significant influence over its actual author(s). As a result, a long list of potential authors has been proposed including Stephen, Barnabas, Apollos, and Priscilla (see Koester, 2010, pp. 42–6). Yet, many Bibles still contain the title of 'Epistle of Paul to the Hebrews'. In this regard, the history of the church and the arguments of biblical scholarship are hardly in unison.

Proof text and interpretative debating ground

Hebrews 1: He is the image of the Father

Hebrews packed some big punches in early Christological debates, as Patristic writers in the fourth century sought to articulate an orthodox Christology (that is, defining the relationship between Christ's divine and human natures). It particularly featured in debates which raged against the Arians. For the Arians (followers of Arius; d. AD 336), the Word was not wholly divine but rather created, and Hebrews featured in the scriptural matrix used to bolster these arguments. For those against these views, a different interpretation was sought.

For example, Epiphanius (d. AD 403) claimed an Arian misinterpretation of the Greek verb *poieó* in Hebrews 3.2: 'having been faithful to the one who *poiēsanti* him'. The Arians interpreted *poiēsanti* as 'having made' (as in Revelation 14.7), rather than as 'having appointed', thus leading to what was deemed an incorrect understanding of the passage (*Panarion* 69.14.1; 37.1, 2). Athanasius (d. AD 373) also flagged the verse as a problematic Arian proof text (*Against the Arians* 2.14.1).

In their refutations of Arian Christology, both writers also draw on Hebrews, particularly Hebrews 1.3 (*Panarion* 72.1, 2; *Against the Arians* 1.3.12) which is full of terms central to debates about the divine nature of Christ: 'He is the reflection (*apaugasma*) of God's glory and the exact imprint (*charaktēr*) of God's very being (*hypostaseōs*)'. The Nicene creed of 381 reflects this anti-Arian position which was ultimately seen as orthodox, and its language resonates strongly with that of Hebrews 1.3 (and 1.2, and more). Therefore, while both sides found Hebrews a potentially convincing text for many of their arguments and counterarguments, Hebrews 1.3 proved particularly pertinent and was seen as so important that it became part of the central declaration of orthodoxy (for more, see Greer, 2011).

Hebrews 6: Those who fall away...

Hebrews 6.4–6 speaks of the impossibility of restoring those 'who have fallen away' (also 10.26–31; 12.17). What exactly this 'falling away' means in practice has been a hot topic for debate for much of Christian history. For the pre-Constantine church of the third century, the passage was invoked in particularly divisive debates. During the edict of Emperor Decius (249–50), Christians who refused to sacrifice to Roman gods were often imprisoned or even killed. Many chose to go into hiding. Others apostatized, and became known as *lapsi*. But when Decius died a year later and the persecution ended, a new question arose: what should happen to those *lapsi* who sought readmission? The matter caused a schism, and Hebrews 6 had a part to play.

For Cyprian (d. AD 258) and his followers, carrying out repentance and penance should mean that *lapsi* could be permitted readmission (Epistle 30). For the followers of Novatian (d. AD 258), passages including Hebrews 6.4–6 formed their 'rigorist' viewpoint which argued that there could be no readmission for these *lapsi*. This echoed the views of Tertullian (d.c. AD 220), who evoked Hebrews 6 to argue that offences including adultery, murder, blasphemy, and apostacy were 'incapable of pardon' (*On Modesty*, 19–20).

But such a rigid doctrine was unpopular with many, to say the least. Thus, while rigorist views persisted, the belief that penance meant that readmission was possible ultimately won the day, and the interpretation of Hebrews 6 as preventing readmission was refuted (Ambrose, *On Repentance*, 2.2). Those who had apostatized could come back into the fold. (For more, see Daly, 1952; Cooper, 2015.)

Hebrews 7: You are a priest forever

For commentators during the Reformation, the discussion in Hebrews 7 of the priesthood was particularly pertinent. Indeed, for those who saw themselves against Rome, this chapter provoked some vitriolic attacks on practices which the Reformers believed were against the message of Hebrews.

For Heinrich Bullinger (1504–75) 'He [Christ] has no need whatsoever for successors' and so 'what need is there for your priestly performance, O utterly shameless Romanists?' (*Commentary on Hebrews*, 7.23–25). John Calvin, in his 1549 *Commentary on Hebrews*, agreed: earthly priests are against the way that the author of Hebrews sees things who, given the import of the topic, must be Paul (7.12). For these commentators, Hebrews 7 is clear: only Christ can be a priest. And yet, they saw the Pope as having set himself up in the order of a priest of succession and a vicar acting as stand in for Christ. Therefore, they viewed priests of this nature, invested with authority, as going against the eternal mediator whose role of permanent priest was made clear through the words of Hebrews 7.24. Indeed, for Bullinger, you are a 'Priest forever' confirms that Christ's priesthood is 'the only necessary priesthood in the world' (*Commentary on Hebrews*, 7.20–22). Therefore, the idea of a Petronic/Aaronic succession was seen as outside the remit of the words of Scripture and 'utterly impudent' according to Calvin (*Commentary on Hebrews*, 7.12).

Within these debates, the words in Hebrews 7 about Christ's priestly position were read by the Reformers as supportive of a break from Rome and thus warranted an entire rethinking of the structure of the church.

Hebrews 8–10: Only a shadow; better

In the late twentieth century, scholars began to explore the rhetoric of Hebrews as part of a wider examination of anti-Judaism in the New Testament. For Rosemary Ruether (*Faith and Fratricide*, 1974), John Gager (*The Origins of Anti-Semitism*, 1985), and Lillian Freudmann *(Antisemitism in the NT*, 1994), Hebrews presented a highly problematic supersessionist picture. And when reading many Christian interpretations of the text from the early church to present day, it is hard to disagree.

Thus, when approaching Hebrews and its problematic reception, it is important to distinguish the text's exegetical drive (to explain a superior covenant) from the history of its effects (how it has created negative attitudes towards Judaism). This is because the language of Hebrews can offer much to those looking for texts to support a break from Judaism. As Alan Mitchell points out: 'the emphasis on a new covenant, often punctuated by the use of the adjective "better," easily lead[s] an unwary reader to conclude that Christianity has superseded Judaism in important ways' (2011, p. 251). As a result, approaching the text today involves looking through two thousand years of Christian interpretative history, much of which obfuscates the complex Jewish nature of the text, which is packed with Jewish-Hellenistic cosmology and in intimate dialogue with the Jewish scriptures. Therefore, scholars are reassessing how it might have been heard by a first-century, Jewish-Christian audience who very much saw themselves as the 'seed of Abraham'.

For example, when considering the frequent use of 'better', Mitchell argues the text's exegetical drive should be understood in relation to the rhetorical technique of syncrisis. In this format, neither item is rendered 'better' than the other but rather each is seen as excellent in and of itself.

Jody Barnard (2014) reassesses the language of 'shadow' (*skia*) in Hebrews, demonstrating how commentators tend to see this as something rendered worthless or denigrated. We see translations reflecting this attitude. For example, 'Since the law has *only* a shadow of the good things to come' (NRSV); 'For since the law has *but* a shadow of the good things to come' (ESV). However, the Greek of Hebrews 10.1 is more accurately rendered as 'The law having a shadow of the good things to come' (Barnard, 2014, p. 38; KJV, RSV) or even: 'For the Torah has in it a shadow of the good things to come' (CJB). Thus, the language of shadow can be understood as producing an outline or a glimpse of what is to come, rather than denigrating the object (the law) itself.

Therefore, reassessing the language and rhetoric of Hebrews can allow us to see the text in a new light and to reconsider what this complex work was saying to its first-century audience, as well as the multiple, and often problematic, interpretative layers which it has since gained.

Seeing Hebrews

Christ the Great High Priest, as outlined in Hebrews, is celebrated alongside his rulership within the Orthodox church in the icon *Christ the Great High Priest/Great Hierarch*. A 1702 example is held in the Alexander Nevsky Crypt Museum in Sofia. This icon states that Christ is High Priest (*Ho Christos Megas Archiereus*), and King of Kings (*Basileus ton basileuonton*). The position of Christ echoes that of Christ Pantocrator but with liturgical additions. He is enthroned, wearing the Eastern Orthodox vestments of an *omophorion* (stole) and *sakkos* (tunic), and he wears a mitre/crown. His right hand is held in blessing and he holds an open book. There is another common variation, where only the top half of his body is visible, as exemplified by the sixteenth-century Cretan artist Michael Damaskenos (Byzantine Museum Athens; inv. no. BXM 13169). Here, the open book displays claims regarding his kingly and priestly status: his otherworldly kingdom (John 18.36) and a call to his body in the Eucharist. Within some churches, images such as these may be found on the back of the despotic (bishop's) throne, making a statement about the power of the one seated beneath this icon. Western traditions have adopted this iconography, but with the alteration to Latin vestments, and sometimes in such examples Christ is shown holding the Eucharist.

The importance of Christ's role and example as High Priest is celebrated in certain parts of the Roman Catholic Church on the first Thursday after Pentecost. This is known as The Feast of Our Lord Jesus Christ, High and Eternal Priest: *Domini nostri Iesu Christi, Summi et Aeterni Sacerdotis*. This is a relatively new feast, first granted in 1987 and since then moving into the proper Calendars of many Conferences of Bishops, including Spain, Australia, and Poland, with the English vernacular being confirmed by decree in 2018 (OLJC 2016; Prot. n. 144/17). Unsurprisingly, readings from Hebrews feature heavily in the day's liturgy and lectionary, with extracts from Hebrews 2, 4, 5, 7, and 10 occurring. Prayers reflect the status of Christ as High Priest and the role of earthly ministers who strive to be conformed in his image.

Melchizedek's priestly role in relation to Christ finds a particular artistic reception in Reformed traditions with Dutch preacher Johannes D'Outrein's extensive commentary on Hebrews published in Amsterdam in 1711. The first volume's frontispiece is an engraving by Jan Goeree (1670–1731). Paul is shown in the centre, looking to a group of men who stand on the left. Their eyes gaze upon what is to the right of Paul: the seated figure of Moses holding the tablets of the Law. Surrounding him are the temple implements. Paul's left hand holds a veil which he has lifted from the face of Moses, and he gestures for the men to look on Moses' face. Shown on the wall behind is the scene of Melchizedek being met by Abraham, with the King of Salem's large retinue visible. This scene was especially pertinent for D'Outrein's arguments, as he presented an innovative thesis that Hebrews 7.3's declaration that the king was 'resembling the Son of God' meant that Melchizedek was not just as a type of Christ, but in fact Christ himself (1711, p. 187). This view was not popular and ended up provoking many debates, but D'Outrein's arguments found an audience, and his immense commentary was even translated into German (Demarest, 1977, pp. 148–9; also de Jong, 2013).

Hebrews 11's list of famous people from Israel's history provides the inspiration for a series of prints by Flemish engraver Pieter Jalhea Furnius (c.1545–c.1626). Furnius created six works, each showing one of the figures mentioned, with their faithful actions demonstrated behind them in the composition. So, in the second work we see Enoch ascending into an open heaven with his garments billowing out in the air while he clasps a large tome under his right arm. In the third, Noah lifts high what appears to be a model of the ark topped by a dove, while in the distance to his right we see the ark on top of a high precipice above the water, the top of which mirrors the model, surrounded with birds, and with animals entering into the ark. In the fifth, Moses holds the tablets of the ten commandments, while in the background we see him holding his staff aloft by the Red Sea as it covers the Egyptians. In the sixth, Rahab is shown with billowing garments, grasping in her hands the cord she will tie in the window, while in the background we see the spies being let down from Jericho's walls. Accompanying inscriptions help to elucidate the faithful actions, each of which is introduced with QUID FECIT. Each concludes with the declaration: FIDES, ending with the central Faith motif for this series.

Thus, this series of engravings allowed viewers to consider the actions of the faithful and look on what it is to have faith.

A different approach to Hebrews 11 and its message of faith can be found in a series of works by New Zealand artist Colin McCahon (1919–87). Between 1979 and 1980, McCahon produced a series of seven works which integrated 'the Letters to the Hebrews' into them. His source was The New English Bible (Simpson, 2023). The artist saw Paul as the hand behind Hebrews and declared: 'I've been rediscovering St Paul & he bowls me over – the letters to Hebrews – they have me in their grip & power & clear honesty. What a guy and what a real message' (Simpson, 2020, p. 317). McCahon's paintings combine monochrome landscapes with painted, cursive script which is taken from Hebrews 11. These works are strikingly textual, drawing on the integral part that words have played in religious art and also exhibiting influence from contemporary sign writing. Yet these works also cause the viewer to look behind the text, to what is in the background.

For example, his 1979 *A Letter to Hebrews* (Museum of New Zealand, inv. no. 1981-0004-1) centres around a giant, brown Tau Cross (a symbol that reoccurs in McCahon's oeuvre) on a black background. Surrounding this symbol are two loose columns of writing in cursive and all caps which recount the actions of the faithful as outlined in Hebrews 11 (in order top to bottom, left to right, they are Hebrews 11.4–15, 1–3, 15–16). The text is painted in white and varies in size and legibility, causing the viewer to engage with and be drawn into the deeds being recounted, particularly in this reordered presentation. Squashed into the top right in more unruly and larger letters, we find two underlined statements: 'it is for their faith that the men of old stand on record' and 'visible came forth'. The text ends in the bottom right with 'for he has a city ready for them'. There is a blank space beneath this text, unbalancing the composition and drawing the viewer towards what appears to be a gently illuminated horizon at the bottom of the work. There is something more to come, it appears, or perhaps something obscured behind the darkness yet to be seen.

In 1980, he made a series of three works dealing with a single verse from the chapter. From this series, *The Testimony of Scripture, No. 2* (1980) features black writing on an orange background, where what appear to be clouds loom at the top, shot through with white. The sky glows and broods. Written across this expanse, the work reads in McCahon's hand, 'By Faith we perceive that the universe was fashioned by the word of GOD So that the visible came forth from the invisible.' A black box anchors the work at the bottom, with a white tau cross punctuating the dark band.

McCahon's compositions of painted text from Hebrews 11 lucidly explore themes of faith and doubt, and in this collection the power of 'Paul's words' inspired him to produce hopeful works, shot through with a sense that like the figures of Hebrews 11, a promised land may be hoped for but perhaps not yet reached, and what can be seen points towards more to come (Evens, 'The Direction I'm Pointing In').

We can see that Hebrews has a strong history as part of Christian worship and theology. It has been central to key debates within the church, often forming part of the arguments of opposing sides as they seek to bolster their positions, a fact which demonstrates the complexity of the contents of the text. It continues to this day to be part of active Christian practice, written in icons and recited in liturgy as congregations consider the role of Christ as Priest and the position of those who minister within the church. And it has been shown that its complex themes and dense arguments can be viewed afresh when artists render Hebrews into something that can be seen, but perhaps not fully grasped.

Recommended further reading

Heen, Erik M. and Philip D. W. Krey (eds), 2005, *Hebrews*, Ancient Christian Commentary on Scripture, NT, Downers Grove, IL: IVP.

Koester, Craig R., 2010, *Hebrews*, Anchor Yale Bible, New Haven, CT: Yale University Press.

Mason, Eric F. and Kevin B. McCruden, 2011, *Reading the Epistle to the Hebrews: A Resource for Students*, Resources for Biblical Study, Atlanta, GA: Society of Biblical Literature.

Peeler, Amy L. B. and Patrick Gray, 2020, *Hebrews: An Introduction and Study Guide*, London: T&T Clark.

Rittgers, Ronald K., 2017, *Hebrews, James*, Reformation Commentary on Scripture, NT, Downers Grove, IL: IVP.

References

Barnard, Jody A., 2014, 'Anti-Jewish Interpretations of Hebrews: Some Neglected Factors', *Melilah: Manchester Journal of Jewish Studies*, 11, pp. 25–52.

Cooper, Derek, 2015, 'What Happens to Christians Who Backslide?', in *Twenty Questions That Shaped World Christian History*, Philadelphia, PA: 1517 Media, Fortress Press, pp. 35–50.

Daly, C. B., 1952, 'Novatian and Tertullian: A Chapter in the History of Puritanism', *Irish Theological Quarterly*, 19 1, pp. 33–43.

de Jong, Henk, 2013, *Johannes D'Outrein (1662–1722)*, Netherlands: Brevier uit-geverij.

Demarest, Bruce A., 1977, 'Hebrews 7:3: A Crux Interpretum Historically Considered', *Evangelical Quarterly*, 49 3, pp. 141–62.

Evens, Jonathan, 2018, 'The Direction I'm Pointing In', in Ben Quash (ed.), *The Visual Commentary on Scripture*, London: The Visual Commentary on Scripture Foundation, https://thevcs.org/question-faith#direction-im-pointing.

Freudmann, Lillian, 1994, *Antisemitism in the New Testament*, Lanham, MD: University Press of America.

Gager, John G., 1985, *The Origins of Anti-Semitism: Attitudes Toward Judaism in Pagan and Christian Antiquity*, Reprint edition, Oxford: Oxford University Press.

Greer, Rowan A., 2011, 'The Jesus of Hebrews and the Christ of Chalcedon', in Eric F. Mason and Kevin B. McCruden (eds), *Reading the Epistle to the Hebrews: A Resource for Students*, Resources for Biblical Study, Atlanta, GA: Society of Biblical Literature, pp. 231–50.

Heen, Erik M. and Philip D. W. Krey (eds), 2005, *Hebrews*, Ancient Christian Commentary on Scripture, NT, Downers Grove, IL: IVP.

Koester, Craig R., 2010, *Hebrews*, Anchor Yale Bible, New Haven, CT: Yale University Press.

Mitchell, Alan C., 2011, '"A Sacrifice of Praise": Does Hebrews Promote Supersessionism?', in Eric F. Mason and Kevin B. McCruden (eds), *Reading the Epistle to the Hebrews: A Resource for Students*, Resources for Biblical Study, Atlanta, GA: Society of Biblical Literature, pp. 251–68.

OLJC, 2016, 'Our Lord Jesus Christ, The Eternal High Priest-Feast (OLJC)', International Commission on English in the Liturgy.

Outrein, Johannes d', 1711, *De sendbrief van Paulus aan de Hebreen*, J. Borstius.

Rittgers, Ronald K., 2017, *Hebrews, James*, Reformation Commentary on Scripture, NT, Downers Grove, IL: IVP.

Ruether, Rosemary, 1974, *Faith and Fratricide: The Theological Roots of Anti-Semitism*, New York: Seabury Press.

Simpson, Peter, 2020, *Colin McCahon: Is This the Promised Land? Vol. 2 1960–1987*, Auckland: Auckland University Press.

———, 2023, 'Peter Simpson on Colin McCahon "The Testimony of Scripture No. 2", 29 May 2023', *Art+object*, 2023, https://artandobject.co.nz/news/peter-simpson-a-testimony-of-scripture, accessed 12.12.2023.

Tradigo, Alfredo, 2006, *Icons and Saints of the Eastern Orthodox Church*, trans. Stephen Sartarelli, Los Angeles, CA: The J. Paul Getty Museum.

Williams, Frank (trans.), 1994, *The Panarion of Epiphanius of Salamis, Books 2 and 3. De Fide*, Leiden: Brill.

7

The Catholic Epistles

KELSIE RODENBIKER

One major question in the reception of the 'non-Pauline Epistles' is whether they should be viewed individually or collectively. As we have seen, traditionally Hebrews has been grouped with the Pauline Epistles. We shall now explore debates about the seven Catholic Epistles concerning whether they should be seen as a New Testament sub-corpus, similar to the 13- or 14- (if including Hebrews) collection of letters attributed to Paul. These Epistles were written throughout a substantial span of possible dates (late first century to late second century), by different people (most obviously James, Peter, John, and Jude, but likely others writing in their names), and for differing reasons. Therefore, this chapter asks, why should we understand these seven letters as a collection if there is no clear, historical tie between their production? We begin by addressing their similarities in content and concerns and their apostolic authorial claims. An examination of shared themes shows the theological connections they share, before a discussion about the reception and acceptance of the corpus reveals the complex process of canonization. We shall also see how their assumed authors have had much to do with their reception and interpretation, thus treating authorship and dating as an essential part of each letter's substance. These letters do much to showcase both the diversity and shared concerns of early Christian writers, and the complexity of creating a body of letters known as canon.

Overview

James

James is introduced as a letter from James, a slave of Jesus Christ, writing to 'the twelve tribes in the Dispersion' (James 1.1). From the opening to Jude, which identifies its author as a brother of James, this James has traditionally been understood as 'James the Just', brother of Jesus and leader of the Jerusalem church (see also Acts 15.1–35; Gal. 2.11–13; Eusebius, *Ecclesiastical History*, 2.23.1–25; Jerome, *On Illustrious Men*, 2). If this letter could be said to have a singular emphasis, it is *integrity*. The author emphasizes the fleeting nature of suffering (1.2–4, 12–16), the instability of doubt (1.5–8), and the ephemerality of wealth (1.9–11; see also Isa. 40.6–8), whereas with God 'there is no variation or shadow due to change' (1.17).

Deeply tied to the issue of integrity is the unjust example of favouritism, particularly regarding wealth disparity (2.1–13). This leads into a discussion about the synthesis of faith and works, and the author is adamant that faith apart from works demonstrates that faith is worthless (2.14–26). Another indication of integrity is the taming of the tongue, as how one speaks expresses their inner being (3.13–18).

These inconsistent 'passions' not only fuel an individual, inward fracturing, and an interpersonal conflict between people, but they also lead to a disconnect between humans and the divine (4.1–12). The author accuses those who would cling to fleeting and fraudulent wealth to the neglect of the labourers and harvesters: 'You have fattened your hearts on a day of slaughter', indicting the wealthy who 'condemned and put to death the righteous one' (5.1–6).

Thus, the author exhorts their readers to be patient for 'the coming of the Lord' like the prophets 'who spoke in the name of the Lord', and Job, who persevered despite severe trials (5.7–11). If anyone suffers, though, the author presents the payoff for those who demonstrate integrity and patience: like Elijah, who 'was a man just like us,' their prayers will be realized (5.13–19).

1 *Peter*

1 Peter is introduced as the letter of Peter, an apostle of Jesus Christ and, similarly to James, is addressed to 'the exiles of the Dispersion', the chosen elect destined to be sanctified by the Spirit (1.1–2). Peter is a key figure throughout the New Testament: chosen by Jesus as the rock upon whom he will build the church (Matt. 16.13–20) and presented by Paul as 'the apostle to the circumcised' (Gal. 2.1–21). Two canonical apostolic letters are attributed to him, offering a theologically comprehensive presentation of Petrine teaching.

This first letter construes an abiding sense of community as essential to overcoming suffering and persecution; suffering is a temporary reality, while the 'imperishable, undefiled, and unfading' inheritance of salvation, foretold by the prophets, is eternal (1.3–12). Like James, 1 Peter empha-sizes the eternal and imperishable nature of 'the living and enduring word of God' (1.22–25; Isa. 40.6–8). The temporality of suffering in contrast to the eternal nature of Christ, salvation, and all that inhabits the realm of God permeates the entire letter.

Salvation, though, is surprisingly paradoxical and connected to suffer-ing: Jesus suffered on their behalf (2.21–25; see also Isa. 53.1–8). Following Jesus' sacrificial example is intended to impact significant human relation-ships such as with political authorities and between enslaved people and masters or wives and husbands (2.13–20; 3.1–13). Because of Christ's suffering, readers are no longer enslaved to their desires but able to live purposeful, clear-minded, and hospitable lives in community with one another (4.1–11). Still, they should not be surprised if they experience suffering – if they share in Christ's sufferings, they may also rejoice in his exultation and glorification (3.14–22; 4.12–19).

Finally, the author exhorts leaders of the community to shepherd their flocks following the example of the 'chief shepherd' (5.1–4) and young people are encouraged to be humbly subject to their elders and patient in suffering, in part as a defence against the wiles of the devil (5.5–9). The author offers a few personal greetings, sends greetings from Mark (the Gospel writer?) and the church in Babylon (that is, Rome), noting that the letter was written through Silvanus (5.10–14).

2 Peter

2 Peter is attributed to Simon Peter (1.1). A self-conscious sequel, this is 'the second letter I [Peter] am writing to you' (3.1), presented as a 'testa-mentary' letter – the last will and testament of an ageing apostle drawing near to his martyrdom in Rome ('Babylon'), as was foretold by Jesus (1.12–15; 5.13; John 21.18–19). Like the author of 1 Peter, this author emphasizes the chosenness of believers (1.1–10; see also, 1 Peter 1.1–12; 2.9–10; 5.13). However, two of the primary concerns of 2 Peter are distinct from 1 Peter: warning readers against being manipulated and misled by false teachers, and the palpable anxiety over the 'last days' (3.3–13).

As one of the 'eyewitnesses of [Jesus'] majesty', the author empha-sizes that 'no prophecy ever came by human will, but men and women moved by the Holy Spirit spoke from God' (1.16, 20–21). The authenti-cation and confirmation of true teaching, for the Petrine author, lies in its source: God. This is in direct contrast to the false prophets and the false teachers, who now present a credible threat to the community through their denial of Jesus, debaucheries, maligning of truth, greed, and deception (2.1–3).

Contrasting pairs of examples from the Jewish scriptural past illustrate the future destruction of these authority-despising teachers: the sinful angels who trespassed from their rightful place versus Noah (2.4–5; see also 1 Peter 3.19–21; Gen. 6) and the cities of Sodom and Gomorrah versus 'righteous Lot' (2.6–8; see also Gen. 19). The unrighteous are doomed to punishment: they subvert the natural order; they 'slander the glorious ones' (2.10–11); their greedy hearts follow the way of Balaam (2.12–18; see also Num. 22–24; Jude 11; Rev. 2.14). The author is clear: these false teachers deserve destruction but the 'godly' will be spared the same fate (2.3).

2 Peter concludes with a discussion of 'the last days'. The 'day of the Lord' will come 'like a thief', and everything will be dissolved and burned away (3.10–13). In anticipation of new heavens and a new earth, what sort of people should readers be? The author exhorts them to be found at peace, patiently leading 'lives of holiness and godliness' (3.11–15), not 'carried away with the error of the lawless' – they should know better, having received this teaching from Peter (3.17).

Jude

Much of 2 Peter's second chapter is drawn from Jude, the last in the canonical order from among the seven Catholic Epistles, which is attributed to Jude 'a servant of Jesus Christ and brother of James' (v. 1). Jude, too, is gravely concerned with the deceit and manipulation of false teachers (vv. 2–4).

Jude also presents contrasting sets of scriptural examples, but in a differing order to 2 Peter and with a few notable exceptions. The positive example of the people saved (by Jesus!) out of Egypt is followed by three negative examples: the unbelievers who were destroyed in the desert, the sinful angels 'who did not keep their own position', and Sodom and Gomorrah (vv. 5–7; see also 2 Peter 2.4; 6, 9; Gen. 19; Num. 14). Michael the archangel provides a positive example: he did not slander *even* the devil (vv. 8–9), but the ungodly slander 'the glorious ones' (v. 8) and so go the way of Cain, Balaam, and Korah (vv. 10–11). Like the false teachers of 2 Peter, Jude's opponents subvert the natural order (vv. 12–13). Enoch is the final positive example: he prophesied the coming of the Lord and the destruction of the ungodly (vv. 14–15; see also Gen. 5.23–24; 1 *Enoch* 1.9). The author of Jude stresses that the teaching of these divisive, ungodly opponents (see also 2 Peter 2.1–3; 3.1–3) can be countered through faith, prayer, having mercy on anyone wavering, and being 'kept' in the love of God (echoing v. 6's angels who 'did not keep' to their place; Jude 17–24).

1 John

Similar to the author(s) of 1 and 2 Peter, the author of 1 John quickly makes known their association to the flesh-and-blood Jesus Christ: 'We declare to you what was from the beginning, what we have heard, what we have seen with our eyes, what we have looked at and touched with our hands', namely Jesus (1.1; see also 4.1–3; 5.6–12; John 1.14). There are many contrasts, similar to the Gospel of John: Christ and Antichrist, light and darkness, truth and lies, love and hatred or fear (see also John 1.1–5).

First, 'God is light', and without God there is only darkness: light, truth, confession, and community are in opposition to darkness, deceit, unrighteousness, and sin (1.5–10). Another contrast is love for the world versus love for God since 'the world and its desire are passing away, but those who do the will of God live forever' (2.17; see also Isa. 40.6–8; John 15.18–25).

Sin presents a paradox. Sin itself is not the problem – claiming to have none is (1.8—2.2). Jesus is an advocate for those who confess their sins, and whose confession leads to a true knowledge of God reflected in their actions (2.3–6). Yet, anyone who commits sin is guilty of lawlessness and no one who abides in God can sin (3.1–9). The author differentiates deadly and non-deadly sins, where only the latter appears to be salvageable through prayer (5.16–18).

The children of God and the children of the devil are revealed in the contrast between those who do right and those who do not (3.10). Light corresponds to love for one another (2.7–11), and love for one another that manifests in substantial and bodily care marks both individuals and communities as abiding in God (3.17, 11–24). Love also fuels belief, and belief leads to action (5.4–5).

Like other authors from among the Catholic Epistles, the Johannine author is concerned with false teaching. False teachers are 'Antichrists' who, despite having come from within the community, deny that Jesus is the Christ (2.18–25). Readers are, therefore, encouraged to 'test the spirits' to determine whether they are from God (4.1). The test is simple: any spirit that says Jesus did come in the flesh is from God; any spirit who says this is not the case is not (4.1–6).

2 John

2 John is not directly attributed to John but rather to 'the elder', writing to 'the elect lady and her children' (v. 1). This letter demonstrates textual overlaps with 1 John, focusing heavily on the imperatives of love, truth, and abiding. The commandment to love one another is not new, the author notes, but one 'from the beginning', that must be lived out (vv. 5–6; see also 1 John 2.7–8). The heart of the letter is a warning: 'Many deceivers have gone out into the world', who do not confess that Jesus came in the flesh (v. 7; see also 1 John 4.1). The elect lady is implored to be careful to discern between those who abide in God and those who do not, and any-one who denies Jesus' incarnation should not be welcomed (vv. 8–11). In the final greeting, the author expresses their desire to be with her in person, and notes that the children of her 'elect sister' send greetings (a possible reference to a church community and their female leader; vv. 12–13).

3 John

The final canonical Johannine epistle is equally brief, again written from 'the elder', this time to 'the beloved Gaius' (v. 1). The author praises Gaius' children who are 'walking in the truth', and his hospitality (vv. 2–8). At the letter's heart is an accusation: the author writes against Diotrephes, 'who likes to put himself first' (v. 9). Diotrephes had been stirring up false charges against the author and their companions, even expelling people from the church who wanted to welcome them (v. 10). On the other hand, Demetrius is spoken of favourably. The author is not subtle in contrasting these figures: 'Whoever does good is from God; whoever does evil has not seen God' (v. 11). Again, the author expresses a desire to be together in person soon, and gives a cryptic greeting from 'the friends', and a request to greet 'the friends there, each by name' (vv. 13–15).

Key themes

Faithful works

The Catholic Epistles collectively emphasize the responsibility of believers to act according to their beliefs – in fact, the connection between faith and action is so inherent, that those who *do not* act faithfully reveal them-selves not to have faith at all.

The second chapter of James is perhaps one of the best-known portions of the Catholic Epistles, in part due to its connection to Pauline passages also dealing, rather differently, with the faith–works debate (compare James 2.14–26 with Rom. 4 and Gal. 3, for example; although see Titus 3.1–3). Taking the examples of Abraham and Rahab, the author says that 'faith by itself, if it has no works, is dead ... For just as the body without the spirit is dead, so faith without works is also dead' (James 2.17, 26). Throughout James is found an imperative of integrity – inward consistency of being – that is reflected in outward evidence through one's actions, especially towards vulnerable people.

Together, the Petrine letters make the connection between living righteously, particularly in difficult circumstances, and following a divine example – for 1 Peter, Jesus' example of suffering selflessly, and for 2 Peter, because God enables participation in the divine nature, which leads to virtuous action.

In 1 John, saying one thing and doing another reveals someone to be living in darkness, sin, and deceit (1.5–10; 2.3–6). Furthermore, the Johannine author implores readers, 'let us love, not in word or speech but in truth and action' (3.11–24, here v. 18).

James and 1 John in particular are not ambiguous: whoever says they have faith, or abide in God, or believe in Jesus but does not *do* anything about it is a liar. They also, in the end, have no faith, because faith and works are two sides of the same coin. Throughout the Catholic Epistles, acting according to one's belief is of paramount importance because it reveals one's true nature.

Stability and endurance

The same integrity – the inner consistency of being – demonstrated by outward acts of faithfulness, such as caring for the vulnerable, not showing favouritism, and being able to rein in one's speech, is also tied to endurance and remaining stable.

The author of James instructs readers to consider their various trials a 'joy' because they test endurance (1.2–4). The inverse of stability and endurance is to be 'double-minded [in Greek, it is literally 'double-souled'] and unstable in every way'. Just as a spring cannot contain both fresh and salt water, or a fig tree cannot grow olives, so also one's behaviour reflects the reality of one's inner being (3.1–10). Likewise, for a request or a prayer to be effective, one must not be internally at war (4.1–10; 5.13–18). James provides a whole network of examples contrasting two modes of being:

unstable, doubtful, and even cruel doublemindedness versus stable, resilient, patient and merciful wholeness, or integrity. Only the whole will last.

As in James, the author of 1 Peter links stability and endurance in suffering. This is all the more pointed because the majority of the letter speaks to the situation of suffering, angling to find amid (and despite) it meaning and purpose. But it will someday be over and readers will be 'established' – stable, enduring, anchored (5.10).

2 Peter warns against manipulation by false teachers who are also called 'the unstable'. Take care, says the author, 'beware that you are not carried away with the error of the lawless and lose your own stability' (3.17). For 1 John, the language of stability manifests as many exhortations to *abide* (2.27–28; 3.6, 9, 14–17, 24; 4.13–21).

Collectively, then, the Catholic Epistles present a substantive concern for the staying power of integrity and stability, over and against the fractured and temporary nature of whatever and whoever is double-minded, unstable, and deceitful – false prophets and teachers, scoffers, and anyone hateful.

'Where is the promise of his coming?'

Anxiety over the 'last days' permeates 2 Peter and Jude, with a brief, urgent declaration from 1 John. Wrapped up in the concern over the last days is the preparation for their arrival and the discernment of related true and false teaching. False teachers, false prophets, scoffers, Antichrists, the ungodly – they bring with them manipulative messages that twist the truth into an unrecognizable, demeaning lie.

For 2 Peter, just as false prophets arose previously, so contemporary false teachers arise (2.1–3). Jude's opponents come 'in the last time ... scoffers, indulging their own ungodly lusts' and causing division (vv. 18–19). To Jude's reminder, 2 Peter adds that they bring ridicule: 'Where is the promise of his coming?' (3.1–7). This is widely interpreted as referring to the alarm over the delay of the Parousia, the return of Jesus after his resurrection and ascension – the 'scoffers' fuel the fire with their mocking words.

Likewise, the author of 1 John warns, 'As you have heard that antichrist is coming, so now many antichrists have come. From this we know that it is the last hour' (2.18). The Johannine author also ties the 'last days' and the proliferation of false teaching (4.1–6). Here the importance of abiding again comes through: 'the anointing that you received from him abides in you, so that you do not need anyone to teach you' (2.27).

As the apostolic authors of the Catholic Epistles are keen to emphasize, truth and discernment are the antidotes to deceitful, manipulative false teaching.

Reception: The canon of Scripture

A sevenfold collection?

One of the key New Testament concepts entwined into the reception of the Catholic Epistles is the construction of the canon and 'collections' of authoritative writings. Debates about what was seen as 'central' and 'peripheral' to the written Christian corpus, and what counted as 'authoritative' for early Christians are brought to the fore when faced with this group of letters. Indeed, their grouping together as a collection, when (as stated in the introduction) there is no clear, historical tie between their production is something worth examining. This is because throughout the early centuries of Christianity many church leaders and writers *did* see these letters as a group, and wrote about them as if they were an intentional collection of letters written by historical apostles. We shall see how this came about.

During the second century, not many were aware of *any* of the Catholic Epistles, but 1 Peter and 1 John are well known and enthusiastically accepted by early church leaders and authors such as Papias, Irenaeus, and Eusebius (see Eusebius, *Ecclesiastical History*, 3.25.2; 3.39.16 (Papias); Irenaeus, *Against Heresies*, 3.16.8; 4.9.2). A possible late second-century composition commonly referred to as the Muratorian Fragment lists just Jude and 1 and 2 John. The earliest material combination of any of the Catholic Epistles was as a part of the Bodmer Composite Codex, an ancient book combining not only Jude and 1 and 2 Peter but also other early Christian and Jewish works written in Greek, including *3 Corinthians* (attributed to Paul), *The Nativity of Mary* (also called the *Protevangelium of James*), and Psalms 33 and 34. Until the major 'uncial' books (written only in capital letters) from the fourth century onward – Codex Vaticanus, Codex Sinaiticus and later Codex Alexandrinus – we have no early material evidence that the Catholic Epistles were a collection. But the writings of church leaders and historians from the same period can shed light on how the Catholic Epistles were grouped in the minds and, perhaps, the practical usage of their readers.

The early history of the Catholic Epistles as a collection is sparse, but in the late third and into the fourth century, church leaders began to refer to certain 'catholic epistles', sometimes referring not to this discrete collection but to letters not written to a specific community, since 'catholic' can also mean 'general'. In the third century, Origen and Clement of Alexandria both use the term 'catholic', but not for a distinct collection of these seven letters. By the early fourth century, Eusebius is the first church writer and historian to refer to James and Jude as two of 'the seven called catholic' (*Ecclesiastical History*, 2.23.25). However, the authoritative status of all seven letters remained up for debate: later Eusebius lists only 1 Peter and 1 John as truly 'accepted'. The remaining five Catholic Epistles – James, Jude, 2 Peter and 2 and 3 John – were relegated to a 'disputed' category due to issues surrounding their 'questionable' authorship (were they really written by who they claimed to be?) and their wide usage by 'the ancients', or earlier church leaders and communities (*Ecclesiastical History*, 3.25.3; see also 3.3.1–4; 3.24.17–18). By the late fourth century, church leaders such as Athanasius (in Greek, in the East) and Jerome (in Latin, in the West) are unhesitating in their inclusion of all seven (and only these seven) Catholic Epistles among the New Testament collection (Athanasius, *Festal Letter*, 39.18; Jerome, *On Illustrious Men*, 1, 2, 4, 9). Jerome acknowledges previous concerns surrounding some of the letters, while Athanasius does not. What is crucial is that over time the Catholic Epistles, despite their earlier disparate production and reception, become understood as an apostolic collection of New Testament letters.

Jumping centuries into the future, modern New Testament scholarship has not necessarily been hospitable to the idea of a sevenfold Catholic collection. It has been common, for the purposes of critical scholarship, to attach the Johannine Epistles to the Gospel of John and Revelation, resulting in a 'Johannine collection' of New Testament works; to combine the study of 2 Peter and Jude, given their similarities; and to treat James and 1 Peter as responses to Pauline writings and theology, rather than their own substantial contributions. Recently, an interest in the collective status of the Catholic Epistles has re-emerged, and with it analyses of, for example, the history of the Catholic Epistles' manuscript tradition, their collective ties to the Acts of the Apostles, and even theological approaches to their coherence as a collection (for more see Schlosser, 2004; Niebuhr and Wall, 2009; Nienhuis and Wall, 2013; Lockett, 2017).

Pseudepigraphy and canon

One key factor in the authoritative status of the Catholic Epistles is the suspicion, both ancient and modern, that they were not written by the apostolic figures to whom they are attributed. In the fourth-century discussions of the formation of the New Testament collection, some church leaders who weighed in on the debate acknowledged that they knew of some works that they did not want to be included because of the question over their authentic authorship – such as James, 2 Peter and 2 and 3 John (see Eusebius, *Ecclesiastical History*, 2.23.25; 3.3.1, 4; 3.25.3; Jerome, *On Illustrious Men*, 1, 2, 4, 9). Athanasius' *Epistula festalis*, 39 from AD 367 takes a different approach. It is a treatise against pseudepigraphy and apocrypha presented as an Easter sermon in which he explicitly accepts all seven Catholic Epistles, but rails against deceiving simple-minded people into believing pseudepigraphal texts are authentic scriptures.

While Jude's authorship appears to be less suspect, that author's reference to Enoch as a prophet is raised as an issue for its authoritative status. Only 1 Peter and 1 John were unhesitatingly accepted as essential to the New Testament collection. But pseudepigraphy – writing in another's name – was a common, creative and strategic literary practice in the ancient world, not a unique 'problem' in the development of Christian writings and collections (for more, see Chapter 5). Even though from early on in their reception most of the Catholic Epistles suffered from suspicion surrounding the 'false' nature of their authorship, the apostolic association to the figures of James, Peter, John and Jude ultimately proved essential to their acceptance among the New Testament letters.

Because James is not cited until the late second century, it is likely that this letter was not written by *the* James, the brother of Jesus and leader of the Jerusalem church (see Acts 15). But there are key details tying the letter *to* James – the address from James 'to the twelve tribes in the Dispersion'; references to the law (see James 1.25; 2.8–12); and the central role of examples from the Jewish scriptural past: Abraham, Rahab, the prophets, Job, and Elijah, making the link both to the figure of James and to the Jewishness of early Christianity. The letter of James also shows significant overlap with Hellenistic philosophical and ethical writing, making it a compelling combination of second-century cultural convergences between Judaism, Christianity, and Greek and Roman literary practices.

There are also at least two 'Peters': one who wrote 1 Peter and the other who wrote 2 Peter. Sometimes it is argued that 1 Peter is an 'authentic' letter of Peter, whether through actual writing by the apostle or by dictation to a scribe called Silvanus who is mentioned in 1 Peter 5.12 (for debates see, for example, Selwyn, 1946, pp. 7–17; Davids, 1990, p. 6; Novenson, 2015; Horrell, 2002). But even if the first letter is authentic, the second cannot be. 2 Peter is generally believed to be the most evidently pseudepigraphal writing in the New Testament: it is starkly distinct in style from the first, combining significant 'Petrine' elements from 1 Peter with the majority of the text of Jude (and possibly other sources such as the *Apocalypse of Peter*). Indeed, David G. Meade claims that 'No document included in the NT gives such thorough evidence of its pseudonymity as does 2 Peter' (Meade, 1986, p. 176; see also Bauckham, 1983, pp. 158–62; Frey, 2018, pp. 217–20). While almost certainly a pseudepigraphal letter, 2 Peter is a strategically Petrine text. It is presented as a self-conscious sequel to 1 Peter, 'the second letter I have written to you' (2 Peter 3.1) that is styled as the last word and testament of an ageing apostle on the way to his martyrdom in Rome (see also 1 Peter 5.13; John 21.18–19). 2 Peter also shows an interesting tendency to alter Jude's scriptural examples (as shown above), removing the references to Michael the archangel and Enoch all together, possibly in the effort to standardize Jude's content with the Jewish scriptures considered popular and acceptable in a Christian context in the mid to late second century. This is fascinating given that Jude's inclusion of Enoch is even noted as 'questionable' by some early church writers, from Tertullian to Jerome, who were interested in delineating the boundaries of the New Testament canon (see Tertullian, *On Female Fashion*, 1.3: Jerome, *On Illustrious Men*, 4).

There are also multiple 'Johns' at play when it comes to the history of the Johannine Epistles. None of these three letters are attributed textually directly to the apostle John. 1 John carries an anonymous address, while 2 and 3 John are attributed to 'the Elder'. Because of this, a variety of hypotheses were proposed by church leaders. For example, Dionysius, a third-century bishop of Alexandria, thought that John really wrote the Gospel of John and 1 John, but that the other two letters might be written by the same 'elder', possibly another John due to there being two monuments to John at Ephesus (see Eusebius, *Ecclesiastical History*, 7.25.1–27). The association to John in these letters is strong, though, both through textual overlap with the Gospel of John and the emphasis on the author's eyewitness experience of the enfleshed Jesus.

In the end, even if *none* of the Catholic Epistles were written by any of their traditional authors, what matters for the history of their interpretation and their reception is that they undeniably *did* become associated with the figures of James, Peter, John, and Jude, and were eventually received as *their* letters. However, this should not be considered a mass deception – as already stated, pseudepigraphy is a widespread and complex ancient literary practice (as seen in Chapter 5). Greek and Roman politicians, philosophers, and poets were commonly employed as creative and strategic pseudonyms, while the writers of many early Jewish works wrote in the names of or for the purposes of expanding tradition related to figures familiar from the Old Testament (or Hebrew Bible) such as Enoch, Abraham, Moses, Job, Isaiah (for examples of pseudepigraphy in ancient literature see, Reed, 2008; Ehrman, 2012; Najman and Garrison, 2019).

The Catholic Epistles remain at the fringes of the New Testament, despite their supposed inclusion in the canon by around the fourth century. This is due to any number of factors. One is the ancient and modern perceptions of their pseudepigraphy. What is more, throughout much of Christian history they have had a subordinate role to the letters of Paul. In addition, their focus on works and practical responsibility has been somewhat unpopular at times. But in the end, these small letters exert a surprisingly large effect on the New Testament and its development. Central to many conceptions of 'canon' is the question of *closure*: at what point was the New Testament collection 'closed', and what books were included in and excluded from that collection? Both the assumption that they played a minor role in the history of the New Testament and the common neglect of the Catholic Epistles are unwarranted. On the contrary, this small and often marginalized group of New Testament letters troubled the very nature of the New Testament collection through their uncertain, pending canonical status for centuries. For readers today, they allow access to essential teachings from early Christianity, particularly in relation to its intertwined relationship with Judaism.

Recommended further reading

Allison, D. C., 2013, *James*, International Critical Commentary, London: Bloomsbury T&T Clark.

Bauckham, Richard J., 2014, *Jude-2 Peter*, Word Biblical Commentary 50, Grand Rapids, MI: Zondervan.

Frey, Jörg, 2018, *The Letter of Jude and the Second Epistle of Peter*, trans. Katherine Ess, Waco, TX: Baylor University Press.

Lieu, Judith, 1986, *The Second and Third Epistles of John*, ed. J. Riches, Edinburgh: T&T Clark.

Lockett, Darian R. (ed.), 2021, *The Catholic Epistles: Critical Readings*, London: Bloomsbury T&T Clark.

———, 2017, *Letters from the Pillar Apostles: The Formation of the Catholic Epistles as a Canonical Collection*, Eugene, OR: Wipf and Stock.

McDonald, Lee Martin and James A. Sanders (eds), 2002, *The Canon Debate*, Grand Rapids, MI: Baker Academic.

Nienhuis, David R., 2007, *Not by Paul Alone: The Formation of the Catholic Epistle Collection and the Christian Canon*, Waco, TX: Baylor University Press.

—— and R. W. Wall, 2013, *Reading the Epistles of James, Peter, John and Jude as Scripture: The Shaping and Shape of a Canonical Collection*, Grand Rapids, MI: Eerdmans.

Williams, Travis B. and David G. Horrell, 2023, *1 Peter*, vols 1 and 2, International Critical Commentary, London: Bloomsbury T&T Clark.

References

Bauckham, Richard, 1983, *2 Peter, Jude*, WBC, Grand Rapids, MI: Zondervan.

Davids, Peter H., 1990, *First Peter*, Grand Rapids, MI: Eerdmans.

Ehrman, Bart D., 2012, *The New Testament: A Historical Introduction to the Early Christian Writings*, 5th edn, New York [u.a.]: Oxford University Press.

Frey, Jörg, 2018, *The Letter of Jude and the Second Letter of Peter: A Theological Commentary*, Waco, TX: Baylor University Press.

Horrell, David G., 2002, 'The Product of a Petrine Circle? A Reassessment of the Origin and Character of 1 Peter', *Journal for the Study of the New Testament*, 24 4, pp. 29–60.

Lockett, Darian R., 2017, *Letters from the Pillar Apostles: The Formation of the Catholic Epistles as a Canonical Collection*, Eugene, OR: Wipf and Stock.

Meade, David G., 1986, *Pseudonymity and Canon: An Investigation into the Relationship of Authorship and Authority in Jewish and Earliest Christian Tradition*, Tübingen: Mohr Siebeck.

Najman, Hindy and Irene Peirano Garrison, 2019, 'Pseudepigraphy as an Interpretive Construct' in Matthias Henze and Liv I. Lied (eds), *The Old Testament Pseudepigrapha: Fifty Years of the Pseudepigrapha Section at the SBL*, Atlanta, GA: SBL Press, pp. 331–55.

Niebuhr, Karl-Wilhelm and Robert W. Wall (eds), 2009, *The Catholic Epistles and Apostolic Tradition: A New Perspective on James to Jude*, Waco, TX: Baylor University Press.

Nienhuis, David R. and Robert W. Wall, 2013, *Reading the Epistles of James, Peter, John and Jude as Scripture: The Shaping and Shape of a Canonical Collection*, Grand Rapids, MI: Eerdmans.

Novenson, Matthew V., 2015, 'Why Are There Some Petrine Epistles Rather Than None?', in Helen K. Bond and Larry W. Hurtado (eds), *Peter in Early Christianity*, Grand Rapids, MI: Eerdmans, pp. 146–67.

Reed, Annette Yoshkiko, 2008, 'Pseudepigraphy, Authorship, and the Reception of "the Bible" in Late Antiquity', in Lorenzo DiTommaso and Lucian Turescu (eds), *The Reception and Interpretation of the Bible in Late Antiquity: Proceedings of the Montréal Colloquium in Honour of Charles Kannengiesser, 11–13 October 2006*, Leiden: Brill, pp. 467–90.

Schlosser, Jacques (ed.), 2004, *The Catholic Epistles and the Tradition*, Louvain: Peeters.

Selwyn, E. G., 1946, *The First Epistle of Peter*, London: Macmillan.

8

The Book of Revelation

MICHELLE FLETCHER

As closings of books go, Revelation's is striking:

> I warn everyone who hears the words of the prophecy of this book: if anyone adds to them, God will add to that person the plagues described in this book; if anyone takes away from the words of the book of this prophecy, God will take away that person's share in the tree of life and in the holy city, which are described in this book. (22.18–19)

These words, which reverberate with Deuteronomy 4.2, make it clear that this text is authoritative and complete. Yet, it is hard to convey just how much Revelation's reception and impact has been shaped by those who have 'added to' its words. Indeed, it is near impossible to approach it today without 'looking through an interpretative lens' created by someone else. There is a reason for this. Revelation is not the most comprehensible of books, and as a result interpretative problems abound: 'How should it be read?'; 'How much, if anything, should be taken as "literal"?'; 'What do its claims about being a prophecy mean for the future?'; 'What do the strange host of characters contained within it symbolise?'; 'How does it speak to the church in the here and now?' In this chapter, we will explore these questions by encountering readers who have wrestled with them. In doing so, we will uncover the rich and varied ways this text has been understood, and the way it has shaped people's lives and worldviews.

Overview

Revelation's author, John, opens his work by making authoritative claims: what he is sharing is from God and Jesus Christ (1.2). John says that he received this revelation on the island of Patmos (1.9) and was instructed to send it to seven congregations in Asia Minor (modern-day Turkey). It begins with him turning to see a strange figure with feet of burnished bronze, a shining face, and a two-edged sword coming from his mouth (1.12–20). This figure has clear Christological overtones (having died, risen, and now ruling), and it is the first form Jesus takes in the book. Seven messages are proclaimed to the seven congregations (2—3) before John is taken up to heaven. Here, he sees the divine throne room, with living creatures, elders and myriads of angels in attendance (4—5).

Within the throne room, a Lamb who has been slain (another guise of Jesus) opens seven seals on a scroll (6; 8), setting into motion cycles of events which wreak havoc on earth, including earthquakes, pestilence, giant hail, and falling stars. Wars break out, including in heaven between the archangel Michael and the Dragon, that is, the devil, leading to the devil and his cohort being thrown down to earth (12.7–9). Strange beasts arise, including one from the sea and one from the land, who forces people to receive the mark of the first beast: 666 (13.18). And signs presaging the approaching end appear, such as a pregnant woman clothed like the sun with the moon at her feet (12.1–6), and seven angels with seven last plagues (15—16). Through all this, it is made clear that the one on the throne is in control and that he and the Lamb deserve praise (e.g. 5; 7; 19). Indeed, the Lamb has his own song (15.3–4), sung by his retinue of 144,000 sealed from the tribes of Israel (7.1–8) who stand with him on Mount Zion.

As Revelation marches into its final chapters, John witnesses the downfall of Babylon the Great, also known as the whore of Babylon (17—18), the defeat of the beasts by Christ in the guise of a rider on a white horse (19.11–21), and the binding of Satan for 1,000 years (20.2). During this time, those who did not receive the mark of the beast come to life and reign with Christ (20.4–6), before the final defeat of the devil and the judgement of all before the throne of God (20.7–15). The text culminates in the descent of the New Jerusalem, a giant golden cube boasting a river, a tree, and the light of God and the Lamb (21—22).

All in all, Revelation is a bewildering read, with frequent narrative interruptions and a vast cast of characters. Therefore, a rewarding engagement requires an open mind, a willingness to go with the narrative flow, and a very good memory.

Key themes

Revealing

Apocalypsis, the opening word of the book, means 'revelation' or 'unveiling', and this is essential for understanding the scenes which follow. From the moment the narrator turns to see the sword-mouthed figure talking to him, the narrative shows that it is conveying its message in 'a different language'. And as multi-headed beasts arise, a woman flies on wings into the desert, and country-sized buildings descend from the sky, the 'other worldly' nature of the text is clear. Thus, Revelation really is a revelation, unveiling things which are not part of the day to day, and conveying messages which purport to show the audience not how things seem, but how they really are. Thus, Revelation's earth-shaking events, battles, messages, and praise unveils to its audience the idea that while their current situation under empire may be difficult, the one on the throne *is* in control and the Lamb has won the victory.

In and out

Within this revealing of how things 'really are', the text is keen to point out who is *not* on the side of the one seated on the throne, and what will happen to them. Thus, a core theme of Revelation is that the battle lines are drawn, and readers need to choose sides now. The messages to the seven congregations make clear that action is required, and that rewards await those who stand firm through all that is to come. What is also clear is that those who choose the wrong side will suffer, and that the enemies of the Lamb will find no reprieve. Therefore, as well as rewards for those who stand firm in Jesus Christ, what will happen to enemies is outlined in gory detail (e.g. 14.9–11; 17.16; 19.20–21; 21.8). The judgement of those who are not found in the Lamb's book of life is eternal, and Revelation's final chapter lists those who will be left outside the New Jerusalem. Therefore, Revelation offers a stark picture of the results of choices made now.

Past and present

Revelation is awash with images from the Hebrew scriptures. To enter into it, is to enter into the world of the 'already seen'. What this means is that while it is often believed to be future-focused, experiences and events from Israel's past ooze from the text. However, Revelation's representation of these images is never the same as what has been encountered before. It does not quote directly, and more often than not, multiple texts and images are woven together, for example within the figure of Babylon and the New Jerusalem. This presents a textual world which is 'altered' from the past, but continually in dialogue. Thus, an important theme of Revelation is that the past continually speaks into the present situation, which is facing its own beasts, trials, and battles (for more, see Fletcher, 2017).

Grand and local narratives

While it can be easy to focus on Revelation's all-encompassing description of the yet to come, it is important to remember that it wasn't written as a time capsule only to make sense to people some 2,000 years later. Revelation was written at a specific time, in a specific place, for specific audiences, and thus an important theme is the localized community within a cosmic struggle. This 'localized narrative' is most overt in the seven messages, each of which is tailored to the seven named locations: Ephesus, Smyrna, Pergamum, Thyatira, Sardis, Philadelphia, and Laodicea. What is more, when John on Patmos saw beasts rise from the sea and all islands flee (16.20) his island-based location seems palpable. Thus, focusing only on the totalizing events overlooks the personal flavour which imbues Revelation. And this specificity should be born in mind when reading the book and as we move to find out how various commentators have interpreted these world-shaking narratives in their own localized contexts.

Reception: Revelation's readings

Reading Revelation

During the first two centuries of the church, Revelation was firmly attributed to John the Apostle and viewed as authoritative. As a result, it was used in works focused on key arguments within the nascent church.

What would happen when Christians died? Revelation 20's descriptions of the first and second resurrection and its millennium were central to debates. Indeed, the earliest extended use of Revelation is in Justin's *Dialogue with Trypho* (c.160), which explains how John the Apostle received a revelation that believers in Christ would dwell for 1,000 years in Jerusalem prior to the resurrection of everyone else (*Dialogue*, 81). This belief in Millennialism, a fast-approaching time of bliss lasting for 1,000 years, was pervasive in the early church. Although theories varied about the period's exact nature (Was it on earth in a restored Jerusalem or in heaven? Did it involve everyone, or just a select few?), Papias (d.c. AD 130), Justin (d.c. AD 165), and Irenaeus (d. AD 200) all had millenarian expectations. This was a source of profound embarrassment for later writers such as Jerome (d. AD 420) who refuted such literalist readings of Revelation, and Augustine (d. AD 430) whose *City of God* sought to delay expectations indefinitely. However, although imminent-expectation understandings of Revelation and a belief in a literal millennium would wax and wane, they would never go away.

In the emerging new movement that was the early church, debates raged about which gospels should be read. Irenaeus tackled the issue by using examples from the earth (four zones, four winds) and Revelation: just as there are four living creatures around the throne of God, so there are four Gospels (*Against Heresies*, 3.11.8). His argument for a fourfold-Gospel has most certainly stuck. So has his alignment of the Gospels with the ox-, lion-, calf-, and human-faced creatures of Revelation 4. Shining in mosaics, glistening in stained glass, and illuminating Gospel manuscripts, this Revelation-rooted identification has become a fixed feature in Christian iconography.

The Antichrist was a key figure in the mindset of the early church. Although the specific term doesn't appear in Revelation, its presence in 1 and 2 John (also attributed to the Apostle) made Revelation a key text in Antichrist-legend development. For example, Irenaeus pinpoints Revelation 13's beast from the sea as this fearsome figure, using the infamous 666 to speculate what his name might be (*Against Heresies*, 5.30.1). For Hippolytus (d. AD 236), the Antichrist was the beast from the earth (*Treatise on Christ and Antichrist*, 2). Differentiations of beast identification aside, the connection between Revelation 13 and the Antichrist have held up across 2,000 years, as any quick Google search will demonstrate (for a comprehensive survey, see McGinn, 1996).

Who are our enemies? Irenaeus and Hippolytus believed that the omission of Dan from Revelation 7's list of the tribes of Israel meant that the Antichrist would emerge from the tribe of Dan, and would therefore be a Jew (*Against Heresies*, 5.30.2; *Treatise on Christ and Antichrist*, 14). This interpretation was a sad parody of Jewish messianic expectations from this tribe, and it begins what becomes a pernicious legacy of anti-Jewish Revelation readings, particularly regarding a Jewish Antichrist. Indeed, it is part of a long-lasting false imposition that somehow Revelation places the Jews on the side of the beast, when in fact it is calling out those who are claiming to be Jews but not living up to those claims.

As engagement with Revelation developed, so too did theories about *how* it should be read and what it was *about*. The fullest manifestations of interpretative strategies appear in the commentary genre.

Victorinus of Pettau (d.c. AD 303) produced the earliest extant Revelation commentary. For Victorinus, Revelation was about the church's relationship with its saviour. But he was concerned about the tribulations found in the text. Would one have to experience these terrible events more than once? No, said Victorinus. He recognized that several sections are very similar, most noticeably the trumpet and the bowl series (Rev. 8; 16) and the actions of the dragon/beast (Rev. 12; 13; 17). Therefore, he asserted that Revelation is not a linear narrative of future events but is recapitulation: more than one description of an event, which allows for a more comprehensive understanding. Thus, he warned that readers' focus should not be on *order* but on *meaning*. This 'let's go round again' way of reading Revelation has proved extremely popular with subsequent commentators, perhaps because it offers a way of bringing internal logic to the tricky narrative.

Imbedded in Donatist debates in north Africa, Tyconius (d. AD 390) produced seven rules for reading. When applied to Revelation, they render it not as an onslaught of eschatology, but as a book focused on the church's own composition and its ongoing fight against enemies, both within and without. Tyconius' rules have a way of eluding exactitude and making scenarios and symbols rather slippery. For example, 'beast' can refer to leaders or the devil or one of its heads or its body (*Commentary on Revelation*, 13.1); 'day of the lord' can mean the time from the passion of Christ, judgement day itself, and a time of persecution (*Commentary on Revelation*, 16.14); Babylon is the city and people of the devil and the vices it is seduced by and seduces with (*Commentary on Revelation*, 14.8). In such a system, it is hard to produce a coherent, 'literal' interpretation. This also applies to his understanding of the millennium, as he confounded imminent expectations by reading Revelation 20's 1,000 years as part of an unspecified time of the church, which will continue until Christ returns. Thus, Tyconius inserted boron rods into Revelation which permitted the force of a future Parousia but averted end-time chain reaction readings. This produced a reading which is always relevant to the now, an indefinite interpretation for indefinite times.

Before chapters and verses, how to structure biblical texts was up for debate. Writing in Greek in the early sixth century, Andrew of Caesarea employed a system to bring order and method to his exposition of Revelation's prophecy. To do this, he uses an image from Revelation's heavenly throne room: the 24 elders. Thus, he divides Revelation into sections (called *logoi*), each of which he then subdivides into three (called *kephalaia*), resulting in the book being split into 72 parts. It is the first extant attempt to carry out such comprehensive systematization of Revelation's text. In doing so, it facilitated section-by-section engagement and provided a rhythm to the reading experience. The form in which we consume a text affects the way we understand it, and later commentators would also consider how to split up Revelation in order to facilitate consumption.

Therefore, in early engagements, Revelation was used in debates about the afterlife, the church's ultimate enemy, and its sacred literature. The first commentaries asserted how the book should be approached, assessed and understood. Andrew of Caesarea became the standard commentary in the Byzantine tradition, and thus the key vehicle through which much of the church later encountered Revelation. In the Latin tradition, Tyconius incorporated Victorinus' recapitulative approach, and Augustine adopted much of Tyconius, propelling recapitulation and the ongoing struggles of the mixed-body church into the centre of Western theology.

Now you see it

Revelation's visual story begins in a similar way to its written one, albeit somewhat later. Early Christian monumental art consisted of highly composite scenes, reinforcing doctrine and cosmology, and declaring peace and power. Revelation-related motifs were incorporated into these awesome compositions, and in the lavish mosaics of fifth- and sixth-century Rome and Ravenna we find scrolls with seven seals, the new Jerusalem, the Lamb on a hill, 24 elders, and Irenaeus's four living creature–evangelists. And it is in the sparkling tesserae of early mosaics that we can perhaps glimpse the chromatic complexity of Revelation at its most sumptuous, with the glistering gold of the holy city, the shining blue of the heavens, and the rainbow around the throne.

Yet, Revelation is not the primary focus of these gloryscapes. It is in a Carolingian manuscript that we find the earliest extant cycle dedicated to Revelation, known as the Trier Apocalypse. Dated to the early 800s, 74 coloured pen and ink drawings accompany the Latin text. Although somewhat less impressive than the Roman mosaics, it is a crucial witness to Revelation's complex illustrated history. For example, despite no accompanying commentary, the drawings exhibit a clear ecclesiastical interpretative lens, as a True Church/False Church, Babylon/Jerusalem polarity runs through its cycle. It also exhibits classical influence in depictions of clothing and beasts. Thus, the Trier Apocalypse demonstrates how interpretative acts affect how Revelation is seen, and how the manifestation of Revelation in the 'now' is always influenced by the past (for more, see Emmerson, 2018, pp. 27–32).

A different kind of visuality and a fresh approach to Revelation sprang from the manuscripts of Joachim of Fiore. Born in the early twelfth century, this monk believed Revelation revealed a holistic order to Scripture and an unfurling of the totality of history. Indeed, he saw it as not only unlocking this totality of history but also containing it. Joachim claimed that his understanding came from images in his mind, and so he used 'figures' (*figurae*) to expound his ideas. These figures, surrounded and filled with text, demonstrated the interpretative lens he was bringing back to Revelation: imminent expectation in the now. For example, in his figure of Revelation's seven-headed dragon, Joachim labels the first five heads as past persecutors of the church, but he makes the sixth head Saladin, the current ruler of Jerusalem. What is more, Joachim believed a new and better age was soon to dawn. He told Richard the Lionheart that his crusade would succeed, resulting in a seven-year reign in Jerusalem (it did not). Nevertheless, Joachim's Revelation-rooted imminent interpretations proved seismic, as Augustine's indefinite focus faced the re-emergence of the definite (albeit a protean approach). Joachim pressed the restart button on the temporal approach to the Apocalypse, and the results still reverberate today.

By the fourteenth century, the illustrated book had become a key medium for Revelation consumption in Europe. Hundreds of costly illuminated manuscripts featuring Apocalypse cycles were created, many replete with the text of Revelation and diverse commentaries in Latin or the vernacular. To experience this form of Apocalypse was a page-turning experience, a symbiosis of text and image, each informing each other. Famous examples include the eleventh- and twelfth-century Spanish Beatus manuscripts and Anglo-French creations such as the Douce (c.1265–70) and Cloisters (c.1330) Apocalypses. Each volume was created to speak to its commissioning audience, be it monks or nuns, kings or queens. For example, in the Trinity Apocalypse (c.1250, fol.14v) we find a woman fighting with a sword against the beast, and in the Welles Apocalypse (c.1310, fol.118r), two portraits of a female face are presented in the text opposite the image of John's vision of the heavenly throne room, instructing its female reader as to how she should become part of the Revelation reading experience. Thus, these books drew their elite readers, male and female, into the world of Revelation, illumination by illumination, explanation by explanation, episode by episode.

Unknown artist, *The Four Evangelists*, ceiling of Mausoleum of Galla Placidia, 425–450, Mosaic, Mausoleum of Galla Placidia, Ravenna, Photo: © MFletcher.

Unknown artist, Apse mosaic showing Christ in Majesty holding a seven-sealed scroll, sixth century, Mosaic, Basilica of San Vitale, Ravenna, Photo: © MFletcher.

Unknown artist, Ceiling showing the presbytery with the Lamb surrounded by four angels, sixth century, mosaic, Basilica of San Vitale, Ravenna, Photo: © MFletcher.

Those belonging to the Benedictine community who met in the chapter house of Westminster Abbey in the late fourteenth century encountered Revelation jumping off the page and on to the walls. Painted in vibrant reds and greens and sparkling with tin and gold adornments, the walls of the chapter house held approximately 96 episodes from Revelation and the life of John. This was still a dialogue between image and word, as vellum was pasted with extracts from Berengaudus's Apocalypse commentary. This choice of exposition provided an interpretation of the text suited to the monastic community. However, unlike the bound prototype, the painting of this cycle on the interior of an octagonal room eschews linearity, as the narrative wraps around the viewer, and to reach the end is to return to the beginning. Such a monumental form renders a truly visceral way to consume the text-shattering proportions of Revelation's unfolding visions.

Within the Coptic and Ethiopian Tawahedo Orthodox churches, Revelation's 24 elders have a special place of honour. From as early as the seventh century, they have appeared in Egyptian worship-spaces, and early examples were present in the monastery of Anba Hatre (St Simeon at Aswan) and the Red Monastery. In Ethiopia, examples include the rock church of Maryam Papaseyti and the church of Abreha wa Atsbaha. These 24 elders are considered incorporeal priests, interceding on behalf of those below and they are attested in Coptic magical papyri, where each was assigned a name corresponding to the letters of the Greek alphabet. Today, their importance is demonstrated through their place in the liturgical calendar, with their commemoration taking place on 24 Hedar/ Hatur (3 December).

The Apocalypse becomes part of the worship space during the Easter liturgy of the Coptic Church. A vigil is held from the evening of Good Friday until the dawn of Bright Saturday, and between the sixth and ninth hour the entire book of Revelation is read aloud. But this is not just a reading of the text. Apocalypse-based responses follow specific verses, including the mentioning of the seven churches (1.9), the tribes and peoples (7.5), Hallelujah (19.1), and stones (22.19). In addition, when incense is mentioned (8.3), the priest responds by lighting incense. In this way, the vigil reflects the heavenly liturgy of worship that occurs within Revelation, as Christ's journey from Hades to heaven is remembered.

In the Byzantine tradition, when it came to depictions of 'last things' Matthew 25-inspired Last Judgements were the preference. However, at the start of the sixteenth century a remarkable Russian icon of the Apocalypse was written for the Kremlin's Dormition Cathedral. Standing at almost 2 metres high, its single panel holds all the action of the Apocalypse, and although divided into different sections, this is not a case of clear progression from left to right, top to bottom. Instead, interconnected scenes travel around the icon, taking the viewer on a heady journey through events. In addition, words are interwoven into the composition, increasing its visual complexity. Its appearance marks a changing attitude to Revelation in the Russian church, and it exhibits influence from Andrew of Caesarea's commentary. More compositions would be produced but few exist (anywhere) which exhibit such single-frame intensity, as temporality slips and slides, events move from earth to heaven to earth again, and the seer and viewer are caught up in the visions (for more, see Anderson, 1977).

Multiplication and multitudes

Most of the interpretations outlined so far were created for a tiny minority, and mostly restricted to monasteries and palaces. However, the proliferation of printing and the upheavals of the Reformation significantly shifted engagements with Revelation, as words and images moved and multiplied.

In 1498, Albrecht Dürer produced a series of woodcuts that would shape the way generations envisioned Revelation. Dürer's compositions pared down the action of Revelation into 14 (15 including the 'life of John' composition) jam-packed scenes creating a highly intense viewing experience. The popularity of his cycle was huge, and the printed medium (and reproductions) allowed the compositions to traverse trade routes. Indeed, we can see their influence in sixteenth-century fresco cycles in Bulgarian, Russian, and Mexican monasteries. They also inspired the compositions by Lucas Cranach that accompanied Martin Luther's 1522 'September Testament'. Cranach's anti-papal renderings made a vivid interpretative point for readers as they sat with the biblical text: the Whore of Babylon and the Beast were the Roman church. As so often had been the case, the 'now' of religious wranglings was firmly reflected in Apocalypse timeline interpretation.

As the text moved into the vernacular and the hands of lay people, so guides were required to assist 'correct' interpretation. Previous commentaries were shunned by Protestants, and so new interpretative strategies were sought. The 'Geneva Bibles' (first full edition 1560) were landmark vernacular print publications, with over 100 versions produced in the sixteenth and early seventeenth centuries. Created by exiled Protestants, it was the first English Bible with verse divisions, and it provided its readers with cross-referencing aids and marginal notes. Revelation could be expounded in a way that 'controlled' readers' imaginations. Thus, rather unsurprisingly, early Revelation notes were anti-papal, and the 1560 edition presented 'Latinus' as the meaning of 666. At the same time, in expounding those included in the New Jerusalem, it affirmed the place of kings within God's system. As its versions progressed, new Revelation-relevant marginalia appeared, and the 1599 version included a full commentary by Huguenot refugee Franciscus Junius. According to Junius, Revelation showed both general history and the history of the church. A helpful table of historical events also accompanied Revelation, with the final date left blank (for readers to fill in?). Geneva Bibles were taken on the *Mayflower* to America, and so their newly coined interpretative marginalia travelled into new geographies and were pored over by new reading communities, who would in turn produce their own interpretations.

Fig 8.4 Albrecht Dürer, The Adoration of the Lamb, from The Apocalypse of
Saint John (1498 Latin edition), 1498, Woodcut on laid paper, sheet: 459 x
312mm, Patrons' Permanent Fund and Print Purchase Fund (Horace Gallatin
and Lessing J. Rosenwald), National Gallery of Art, Washington, 2008.109.14,
Courtesy National Gallery of Art, Washington.

Figure 8.5 Albrecht Dürer, The Seven Angels with the Trumpets, from The Apocalypse of Saint John (1498 Latin edition), 1498, Woodcut on laid paper, sheet: 458 x 311mm, Patrons' Permanent Fund and Print Purchase Fund (Horace Gallatin and Lessing J. Rosenwald), National Gallery of Art, Washington, 2008.109.8, Courtesy National Gallery of Art, Washington.

At the close of the sixteenth century in Scotland, embroiled in fraught Catholic–Protestant politics, John Napier (1550–1617) sought to apply logic to the world. He discovered logarithms. And he set out to decode Revelation. Napier believed the Apocalypse was an exact system, and that this system could be used by the right persons (him), to plot the exact course of history up until the 'now', potentially even predicting the future. Napier produced a concrete dating system of set points at equal distances: find the past events which matched the dates and all key moments of history would be brought to light. The specificity of Napier's approach and method of conveyance was unique. Where Joachim had *figurae*, Napier used a cutting-edge medium already employed by the Geneva Bible: the table. He placed his interpretations in columns next to Revelation's text, lining up the messages and showing the 'logic'. However, although covering millennia, Napier's interpretations were deeply parochial, including current familial crises in Revelation's timeframe. The first print run addressed King James I, hoping to persuade the monarch to the interpretation. It did not. But Napier's precise calculating interpretations still spread and bred, appearing in Dutch, German and French, and being republished in England as puritan mentalities grew (for more, see Havil 2014). Other (deeply parochial) explanations of the Apocalypse as a plottable imminent prophecy followed, including Joseph Mede's highly influential 1627 *Clavis Apocalyptica* ('Key to the Apocalypse'). These time-spanning, 'now-flattering' works became part of the reading material of those who sought to expedite the end times in 1649 by killing King Charles I. Impactful indeed.

Counter-Reformation interpreters took a different approach. Jesuits Francisco Ribera (1537–91) and Robert Bellarmine (1542–1621) argued that Revelation spoke of an unknown time in the future where the Catholic church would fall into apostasy, while Luis de Alcazar (1554–1613) saw it as a great tale of the church's triumph, with intimations of its ultimate consummation. At the same time, the Council of Trent's debates about Mary's sinless nature created a Revelation-rooted iconography which would proliferate around the world: the Immaculate Conception. The identity of Revelation 12's Woman Clothed with the Sun has often been read as Israel, or the church, but Mary had also been considered as the figure since the fifth century (e.g. Quodvultdeus, *De symbolo* 3). However, Immaculate Conception discussions took this identification further, particularly within Spain. Thus, it was a key doctrine for the orders who first went to the Americas, particularly the Franciscans, and its popular Revelation 12-infused iconography was transported. A testament to its spread and localized transformation can be seen today in Quito, Ecuador.

Set against a backdrop of Andean peaks is the world's tallest aluminium statue: the Virgin of El Panecillo (designed in the 1970s by Agustín de la Herrán Matorras). She is a striking, silvery-winged figure with a ring of 12 stars above her head and her right hand raised in blessing. She is dressed in a floor-length robe and on her chest is a small, radiating sun, while under her feet is both a crescent moon and a coiled serpent. Based on the 1730s *Virgin of Quito* carved by Ecuadorian Bernardo de Legarda, her monumental presence above the city speaks of the relevance of the iconography for this specific place: this is *Quito*'s Virgin of the Apocalypse.

A similar vernacular testimony can be found in our Lady of Guadalupe, Mexico City's sacred symbol. Also resonating with the Woman Clothed with the Sun, our lady of Guadalupe (whose story dates to 1531) has been a key symbol of identity for central Americans and remains so today (for more, see Sanchez, 2008). Yolanda López's 1970s 'Guadalupe series' features three generations of her matriarchal family. The artist wanted to use the Guadalupe iconography to show the strength of Chicana women, and each portrait reveals a woman who is self-sufficient and aware of their own power. Thus, in Lopez's renderings she and her forebears are a *woman* clothed with the sun, speaking directly and specifically for and to women today. (For more, see O'Hear and O'Hear, 2015.)

Joanna Southcott (1750–1814) went a step further than Lopez; in an 1801 publication, she declared herself to *be* the Woman Clothed with the Sun. Born in Devon in south-west England and having worked in farming and domestic service, Southcott received revelations in her forties which set her on a life-changing course. Amazingly, the testimony of this woman was taken seriously, and her writings revered (she was purported to have 100,000 followers in 1814). The 'Southcottians' were formed, and in 1804 selected revelations were sealed in a box, to be opened by 24 bishops (echoing the 24 elders) in a time of national danger. Her role as the Woman Clothed with the Sun took itself to another level when the 64-year-old virgin showed signs of pregnancy, declaring that she was about to give birth to the messiah Shiloh (based on Gen. 49.10). It was a phantom pregnancy and Joanna died soon after. But various Southcottian groups would claim to be her successors and create new versions of belief (for more, see Court, 2008, pp. 131–8). Even today her legacy lives on, with ex-MI5 agent turned self-declared messiah David Shayler believing himself to be Shiloh (see Bendiksen, 2017). Joanna was a pioneer of the independent religious group who used the power of Revelation to create a firm following.

Another woman who harnessed the power of Revelation was Ellen G. White (1827–1915). White was a central figure in the founding and development of the Seventh-day Adventists whose eschatological teaching evolved from the teachings of William Miller (1782–1849). Miller used an amalgam of Bible passages to predict Christ's second coming and the start of the millennium. His preaching proved extremely popular, but when the events failed to manifest (first in 1843 and at a revised date of 22 October 1844), some followers went about reconsidering what this seeming let-down meant. White was a central part of this when in December 1844, she received her first Revelation-filled vision (many more would follow), seeing a sealed 144,000 Adventists being led to the Holy City. Subsequent visions showed her that Jesus had entered the holy of holies in 1844 where he would leave with the seven last plagues once his work was completed. Her influential writings, brought together in *The Great Controversy* (1888), expounded early Adventist beliefs and argued that the 1755 Lisbon Earthquake, the darkening of the day and a blood-red moon in New England in 1780, and 1833 sightings of the Leonids meteor showers were the sixth seal of Revelation, thus showing these were the last days. Through her visions and writings, White turned the exactitude of Miller into imminent expectation. Despite its often-localized focus, this eschatological approach appealed to many and today Adventism is a global movement, with around 25 million adherents, while White's writings remain hugely popular and widely translated.

In 1909, the publication of the Scofield Reference Bible led to a return of annotations heavily influencing Revelation. In the nineteenth century, American Protestants placed a strong emphasis on the 'self-sufficient' nature of the Bible. Indeed, the American Bible Society had a policy of producing Bibles that had no additional notes or comments included. But biblical interpretation was a challenge for many readers, and so lawyer-turned-preacher Cyrus I. Scofield sold a solution: his annotated Bible. Scofield purported that with the right tools, the 'self-contained system' within the Bible could be categorized and revealed: all you need to see it is a Scofield Bible. The 'right tools' were the interpretative methods of the growing dispensationalist movement (for example, types, numerics, and chain references) who believed that there was a scientific nature to the Bible and thus a system behind the text (see Pietsch, 2015, pp. 96–124). Revelation was pivotal within this system as the concluding part of the progressive unveiling of Scripture: a map for what was, is, and is to come. Scofield's succinct notes proffered clarity, bringing seeming order when set beside Revelation's writhing textual action and including a seven-point end-times schedule to accompany Revelation 20. Within this schedule, Scofield placed 'rapture' before a period of tribulation. In doing so, this relatively nascent idea of 'pre-tribulation rapture' became an integral part of the roadmap for the future. Scofield's easy-read references and a heavy marketing campaign led to amazing sales and many subsequent versions which furthered dispensationalist reading strategies. What is more, the 'self-contained' nature of Scofield's Bible appealed to the growing American foreign missionary enterprise, and as a result these far-from-mainstream methods of Revelation reading dispersed around the world. This has had an enormous interpretative impact, reverberating in many forms of global Christianity today.

Figure 8.6 Agustín de la Herrán Matorras, *The Virgin of El Panecillo*, 1970s, Aluminium sculpture, El Panecillo, Quito, Ecuador, Photo: Diego Delso CC BY-SA delso.photo.

During Apartheid in South Africa, Allan Boesak discovered an interpretation of Revelation which spoke powerfully to the 'now' being faced by black South Africans. In *Comfort and Protest* (1987), Boesak argued that Revelation should be read as first-century protest literature written for a persecuted minority. He asserted that it does not present a roadmap for the future, and that debates about compositional dating and emperors should not be the focus. Instead, Revelation's potency lies in a time-transcending message for the destitute and oppressed – that there is a God above the gods of oppression; a political message just as relevant for the Israelites in Egypt, as it was for the prophet on Patmos, as it is for the struggles against evil today. From this perspective, Revelation reveals evil systems (for example, the first beast is the corrupted and illegitimate state; the second

REVELATION

is the theological justification for the first), and it demonstrates how beasts will arise again and again (Hitler and Apartheid being examples). What is more, it calls readers not to submit in silence but to resist the systems of violent oppression which destroy the earth, enslave the weak, and starve and kill the vulnerable. Thus, Boesak found a message which he believed could only be truly understood by those enduring these evil systems, those facing imprisonment and death. Boesak's reading renders Revelation a text alive with political critique, offering comfort and hope to those facing the unbearable 'now', and sharp rebuke to those who silently look on. In this interpretation, Revelation is not a puzzle to solve, a vision to behold, or a future to simply wait for, but a book which speaks directly to the destitute and oppressed, an interpretation of Revelation which Boesak confesses 'forever changed my life' (1987, p. 11).

Recommended further reading

Boxall, Ian, 2002, *Revelation: Vision and Insight*, London: SPCK.
Chilton, Bruce, 2013, *Visions of the Apocalypse: Receptions of John's Revelation in Western Imagination*, Waco, TX: Baylor University Press.
Court, John M., 2008, *Approaching the Apocalypse: A Short History of Christian Millenarianism*, London: I.B. Tauris.
O'Hear, Natasha and Anthony O' Hear, 2015, *Picturing the Apocalypse: The Book of Revelation in the Arts over Two Millennia*, Oxford: Oxford University Press.
Weinrich, William C. (ed.), 2006, *Revelation*, Ancient Christian Commentary on Scripture, NT, 12 Downers Grove, IL: IVP.

References

Anderson, Caryolyn Willson, 1977, 'Image and Text in the Apocalypse Icon of the Dormition Cathedral of the Moscow Kremlin', Unpublished PhD, University of Pittsburgh.
Bendiksen, Jonas, 2017, *Jonas Bendiksen: The Last Testament*, illustrated edition, New York: Aperture.
Boesak, Allan Aubrey, 1987, *Comfort and Protest*, Philadelphia, PA: Westminster Press.
Court, John M., 2008, *Approaching the Apocalypse: A Short History of Christian Millenarianism*, London: I. B. Tauris.
Emmerson, Richard K., 2018, *Apocalypse Illuminated: The Visual Exegesis of Revelation in Medieval Illustrated Manuscripts*, University Park, PA: Pennsylvania State University Press.
Fletcher, Michelle, 2017, *Reading Revelation as Pastiche: Imitating the Past*, London: Bloomsbury T&T Clark.

Havil, Julian, 2014, *John Napier: Life, Logarithms, and Legacy*, Princeton, NJ: Princeton University Press.

McGinn, Bernard, 1996, *Antichrist: Two Thousand Years of the Human Fascination with Evil*, San Francisco, CA: Harper.

O'Hear, Natasha and Anthony O'Hear, 2015, *Picturing the Apocalypse: The Book of Revelation in the Arts over Two Millennia*, Oxford: Oxford University Press.

Pietsch, B. M., 2015, *Dispensational Modernism*, Oxford: Oxford University Press.

Sanchez, David A., 2008, *From Patmos to the Barrio: Subverting Imperial Myths*, Minneapolis, MN: Fortress Press.

Weinrich, William C., 2005, *Revelation*, Ancient Christian Commentary on Scripture, NT 12, Downers Grove, IL: InterVarsity Press.

Weinrich, William C. and Thomas C. Oden, 2011, *Greek Commentaries on Revelation*, Downers Grove, IL: Inter-Varsity Press.

———, Thomas C. Oden and Gerald L. Bray, 2011, *Latin Commentaries on Revelation*, Downers Grove, IL: Inter-Varsity Press.

Index of Names and Subjects

Printed in the USA
CPSIA information can be obtained
at www.ICGtesting.com
JSHW020230011124
72662JS00004B/31